what's my name?

siamese sit-down

balloon football

squirrel-in-a-tree

THE **REAL BOOK** OF
Games

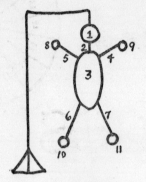

EDITED BY HELEN HOKE

GARDEN CITY BOOKS, GARDEN CITY, NEW YORK
BY ARRANGEMENT WITH FRANKLIN WATTS, INC.

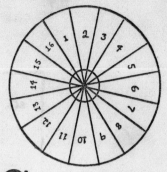

THE Real Book OF

Games

by JOSEPH LEEMING

illustrated by IDA SCHEIB

Contents

5

Foreword

HERE are all kinds of games—games to put party guests at ease, indoor and outdoor games, games that are good for small groups and perfect to get large ones together, noisy and quiet games, games for picnics and beach parties—and games for just about every occasion!

Some people think the most needed part of this book is the section on games for two people. How many times have you and a friend been at your wits' end for something interesting to do? You'll find this a good book to keep at hand for exciting ideas to help fill empty hours.

Each game in this book has been carefully chosen. Each one has proven popular with young people, is easy to play and requires no special equipment or preparation.

This book has been written to help you enjoy your free time. All the games described in it, new or old, have given hours of amusement to thousands. And you and your friends should find them fun, too.

JOSEPH LEEMING

THE **REAL BOOK** OF
Games

Icebreakers

IT'S OLD STUFF to say, "I can't have a party because my friends don't know each other."

Enough of that! It's strictly up to you, as host or hostess, to see that they get together. So send out your invitations, and when your guests arrive, start them mixing *fast* with one or two of these sure-fire Icebreakers. When all the newcomers get into the party spirit and become part of the group, they'll start having a wonderful time.

These games are just as exciting for old friends sitting around like Gloomy Guses at a party as for those who don't know each other. They're guaranteed to start the fun off with a bang!

11

MIX

This is a good active icebreaker that brings everybody into the group very quickly.

The host asks everyone present to listen to him and says, "When I say 'Mix into twos,' each of you stand with someone else and make a pair. When I say 'Mix in threes, fours or fives,' get into groups of three, four or five. Got it?"

He then gives directions. The party will get very lively as people scurry around to make the right-sized groups. In a set of Mix one or more persons will be left out. That is all right. They form a group by themselves and wait for the next turn.

LEFT-HANDED AUTOGRAPHS

Each player is given pencil and some paper and is told to go around to the others and ask them for their autographs. Everyone (except lefties, who do the reverse) must write his autograph with his left hand. This is always fun! Keep the autograph hunt going as long as everybody is amused and enjoying it. Don't make it a rule that each player has to get the autograph of every other player, though! If you see your guests becoming restless, start a new game.

SECRET PENNIES

Two or three players are secretly given a few pennies, which they conceal in their right hands. The host then tells the guests to circulate and shake hands with everybody else. He adds: "Watch out for a big surprise."

Everybody shakes hands and those who have pennies pass them secretly to the *tenth* person with whom they shake hands. They ask these people quietly to give the pennies to the tenth person with whom *they* shake hands. As soon as the game has achieved its purpose of getting the guests talking and laughing, the host calls a stop to it. Then he explains what it was all about and tells the people who are then holding the pennies to keep them as good-luck pieces.

CINDERELLA'S SLIPPER

To pair off boys and girls for an evening, ask each girl to remove one of her shoes. All the shoes are mixed together and put in a pile at one end of the room. The boys then line up at the other end of the room. At a signal they run to the pile and each one picks up a shoe. Then they run back and find the girls who are wearing the matching shoes.

13

DIVIDED PICTURES

Use this icebreaker to start people moving around and meeting others by giving each guest one-half of a picture that has been cut in two and telling him to find the person who has the other half. (Use colored advertisements for the pictures.)

Cutting the pictures in two is a good method to use if you want boys and girls to pair off as partners. (Be sure you distribute the halves carefully.) But if you wish to use this stunt to make a lot of people acquainted, you can cut each picture into four, six or eight pieces. Then a whole group will have to get together to match the different pieces.

PEANUT COLLECTING

Each person is given several peanuts, and is told to hide them in his hands. The boys then go to the girls, hold out their hands, and say, "Odd or even?" If a girl guesses correctly whether a boy holds an odd or an even number of peanuts, she gets his peanuts. If the girl guesses incorrectly, the boy gets her peanuts. Set a limit of five or ten minutes for this game. Whoever gets the most peanuts by the end of this time is the winner.

NAME RHYMES

Here is an especially good icebreaker for a group in which there are quite a few people who don't know each other well. Each player stands up and tells his first name together with a brief rhyming description of himself. For example:

"I'm Dick, and my head's pretty thick."

"I'm Grace, hope you like my face."

It is hard to find rhymes for some names. In such a case the player is allowed to use his last name or else say something like:

"Gladys I'm named, and I hope to be famed."

"Elmer I'm called, and I'm glad I'm not bald."

FISHING

This game is most fun to play when there is an equal number of boys and girls. The girls go into a room next to the room in which the party is being held and hide behind the door, which is left open a few inches. One boy then takes a string with a pencil or some other small object tied to its end, and throws it through the opening of the door. One of the girls grabs it and is "caught." She comes back into the room. Each boy gets a turn until all girls are caught.

WHAT'S MY NAME?

When all the guests have arrived, pin to each guest's back a slip of paper with the name of a famous person written on it. No one is told what name is on his back. The guests have to try to find out their names by asking the other players questions.

Players may not ask the same person more than one question at a time, and may ask anything but "What's my name?" They must keep moving from one person to another. This is what makes this game one of the best of all the icebreakers.

WHO AM I?

This is a variation of "What's My Name?" It gets everybody mixing and talking right away.

Before the party, write the name of each guest on a piece of paper, and after everyone has arrived, pin a name on each person's back. Pin the boys' names on the girls' backs, and the girls' names on the boys'.

The players then try to discover who they are by asking only such questions as can be answered with a yes or no, and do not require anybody's name to be mentioned. Questions about other people's clothing are not allowed, since that would make it too easy.

When a player thinks he has found out whose name he has, he may ask if he is right.

SING A SONG

Choose several songs that you are sure everybody at the party will know. Write a line of each song on a separate piece of paper. When the guests arrive, give each one of them one of the slips, and tell them it is up to them to find the others who have lines of the same song. When all the ones who have the same song find each other, they are to sing the song. The group that sings its song first wins.

COLLECTING NAMES

This icebreaker should not be started until all the guests have arrived. When they are all present, pin a piece of paper with a name written on it to each guest's back. The names may be those of movie stars or other well-known or famous people.

Now give each guest pencil and paper and tell them to see how many of the other guests' names they can write down, while hiding their own name from view. Standing with your back against the wall in order to hide your name is not allowed. The result is that everybody moves around sideways and uses every possible means to keep people from getting behind him.

Ten or fifteen minutes should be allowed for the name hunt, depending on the number of people. The player who gets the most names is one winner, and the player whose name appears the fewest number of times on all the lists is the second winner.

Active Indoor Games

THESE aren't quite as roof-raising as the Boisterous Games you'll find later on, but they're easier on the furniture, and still pack a lot of fun.

Among the games in this section you'll find several old favorites, and some new ones for you and your friends to try out. They're terrific for two or twenty —or even a whole house full.

RHYTHM

Everybody sits on the floor in a circle. Then the group starts to beat time, to get a rhythm going. First they slap their hands on their knees once, then clap their hands together once, then slap their hands on their knees again, and so on. They keep this up for about a minute and then someone—it may be anyone —calls out a word, and the game begins.

Let's say that someone calls out the word "smile." The group then goes through the rhythm of slapping knees, clapping hands, and slapping knees again. Right after the last motion, the player sitting to the right of the one who called the first word, must call out a word beginning with the *last letter* of the first word. In this case, the player could call out "elephant." The group then goes through the three motions again and the next player to the right may call out "train."

The game is most fun when it is played fast. The rhythm is kept up like this: clap, clap, clap, word; clap, clap, clap, word; and so on.

You aren't allowed to use names of persons or places. When a player misses three times, he is eliminated. A player can miss by calling out the name of a person or place, or by failing to call out a word immediately after the last beat of the rhythm.

21

WHO IS NEXT?

This game is a lot of fun when played fast.

The players sit on chairs and sofas in their usual positions in the room. One player starts the game by pointing a finger at someone else, calling him by name, and saying, "Who is next?"

If the first player points with his *right* hand, the other player must point immediately to the player on his right, call him by name, and say, "Who is next?" But if the first player points with his *left* hand, the second player must point to the player on his left.

The second player, of course, may point in his turn with either hand, and the player he points to must follow his signal correctly.

Someone is sure to get confused before long and point in the wrong direction. When this happens, the player has one point scored against him. After a player has three points scored against him, he must drop out of the game. The game keeps on until only two players are left, and they are the winners.

BARNYARD CHORUS

This is not exactly a game of skill, but it does provide a wonderful excuse to make a lot of noise!

One player starts by saying that he has some cows. He starts to moo. Another player says he has some roosters and immediately begins to crow. The other players then tell what animals they own and start to make the right—or nearly right—sounds for those animals. When everybody is going at full blast, trying to drown out his neighbors, the Barnyard Chorus is really something to listen to.

Barnyard animals that can be imitated include sheep, mules, pigs, horses, ducks, goats, dogs and cats. Players can also imitate birds, frogs and crickets.

BLIND MAN'S BUFF

One player is blindfolded and given a cane or stick. The others, hand in hand, walk in a circle around him. When the Blind Man claps his hands three times, the others stop moving.

The Blind Man points his cane toward the circle, and the player to whom it points must take hold of it and make three sounds asked for by the Blind Man. These may be to bark like a dog, crow like a rooster, meow like a cat, sneeze, laugh or yodel. The player does everything he can to disguise his voice, and the Blind Man tries to identify him. If he succeeds, the other player becomes the Blind Man.

SUBMARINE

This is an active game but, strangely enough, the winning team is the one that is the quietest.

To get ready for the game, two chairs are placed facing each other and about eight feet apart. Two players are blindfolded and seated on the chairs facing each other. They represent radar stations. The space between them stands for the Strait of Gibraltar or some other narrow body of water.

The rest of the players divide up into two equal teams. At a signal from the leader, one player from each team starts out on tiptoe to try to pass silently between the chairs. These players are submarines.

If either one of the blindfolded players hears a sound, he says so and points to where he thinks it came from. If he is right, the player he points to is "sunk." If he points in the wrong direction, the submarine goes ahead at slow speed. The team that gets the most submarines safely through the strait is the winner. Each team goes through just once.

FOLLOW ME

This game is best for about fifteen players.

All players sit on chairs or stand in a circle except

"It," who stands in the middle. When the game starts, all the players hold their left hands out in front of them.

"It" starts walking around the circle. Pretty soon he takes hold of someone's left hand, and that player follows him, holding his hand. This player takes someone else's hand, and the line keeps growing in length.

Suddenly "It" shouts "Scoot!" and runs for a place in the circle. All the others in the line dash like mad to get themselves a place. The last player to reach the circle—or get a chair—becomes the next "It."

MONKEY

This game can only be played once by any group, but it is a very funny one for a large party.

The players sit around the room, and the leader (the only one who knows the game) gives each one in turn the name of an animal. He tells each one to keep his animal name secret.

When he has gone around the room, he says that he has given the same name to at least two people. Then he puts an orange or an apple on the floor in the middle of the room and calls the name of an animal. The players with that name run to pick up the orange. The first one to reach it is given the orange, and another orange is put on the floor in its place.

Now comes the joker. The leader has given nearly all of the players the name "Monkey." After he has called two other animals, he calls "Monkey!" There is a wild stampede for the center and everybody gets a big surprise.

SEATED BLIND MAN'S BUFF

This is an unusual version of the regular "Blind Man's Buff." The players sit in a circle, either on chairs or on the floor, and a blindfolded player stands in the center.

The blindfolded player waits for about a minute while the other players change places, taking care not to talk or laugh so the Blind Man can identify them. The Blind Man then calls "Stop," and steps up to one of the players and feels his face. He tries to guess who the player is by passing his hand over the player's face and hair. If this doesn't work, the Blind Man can ask a leading question and the player must answer it in a whisper.

If the Blind Man guesses who it is, the other player becomes the Blind Man. If he doesn't guess, he must try another player, and continue the game until he identifies someone.

26

PASS THE THIMBLE

This game is something like "Button, Button, Who's Got the Button?" Try it the next time you're with a group of ten or more who want something that's fun to do.

The players sit in a circle, on chairs or on the floor. "It" stands in the center. Each player in the circle grasps with his left hand the right wrist of the player sitting at his left. This takes the left hands out of action, but leaves the right hands free. One of the players has a thimble, a button, a penny, or any other small object.

Each player, in turn, puts his right hand first in the right hand of the player on his right, and then in the right hand of the player on his left. Everybody sings this verse to the tune of "The Campbells Are Coming":

The thimble is passing from chair to chair,
It's here and it's there, and I don't know where.

The player in the center watches everybody's hands very carefully. Finally, he will see something suspicious and will think he knows who has the thimble. He points at this person. If he has guessed correctly, the player who has the thimble goes to the center, and "It" takes his chair in the circle. But if he does not guess the right player, he has to try again.

DO THIS, DO THAT

The players are seated around the room, and one player, who is the leader, sits or stands where everybody can see him.

The leader starts, for example, by holding one ear and saying, "Do this!" Every player must immediately do the same thing. Then the leader does other things, which the other players must imitate. He may clap his hands, stretch his arms out to the sides or over his head, raise one foot from the floor, move his hand in a circle, pat his head or stamp his feet.

The trick is that when the leader says, "Do that!" instead of "Do this!" the players must do nothing. Any player who copies his actions must drop out or have a point scored against him. At the end, the player with the lowest score is the winner.

DEER HUNT

There is no other game quite like "Deer Hunt." It gives the players the eerie thrills of taking part in a blindfolded chase.

Two people—the Deer and the Hunter—play at one time, while the others watch. The Deer and the Hunter are blindfolded and are then led to opposite ends of a long table such as a dining-room table. At the signal to start, they begin to move around the table, touching the table at all times with one hand.

The object of the game is for the Hunter to catch the Deer. Both of them move silently, on tiptoe, or the Hunter may make a quick dash if he hears the Deer moving nearby. The players can move around the table in either direction, and can reverse their direction any time they wish to. The game is as exciting to watch as it is to play.

STIR THE SOUP

There should be about ten players to make "Stir the Soup" go with a bang.

The players sit on chairs in a circle. There are just enough chairs for all the players with the exception of "It." "It" stands in the center, holding a cane, umbrella or stick.

To start the game, the players leave their chairs and form a circle around "It." Then they walk around the circle, telling "It" to "Stir the soup! Stir the soup!"

"It" makes the proper motions with his stick to give the soup a good stirring. Then, all of a sudden, he taps the floor three times, drops the stick, and makes a dash for a chair. All the others run for a chair, too. But one player is bound to be left out, and he becomes the new "It."

HOLD FAST! LET GO!

Five people can play this game at one time. If you play it at a party where there are a lot of people, divide up into groups of five. In each group there are four players and one leader.

One of the players offers his handkerchief for the

game, and the four players hold the corners of the handkerchief. The leader then calls directions, and the players must try to do the exact *opposite* of what he tells them.

The leader uses two commands—"Hold fast" and "Let go." When he says "Hold fast," the players must let go and drop the handkerchief. When he says "Let go," they must hold fast. It is very confusing!

When a player makes a mistake he drops out. Finally, only one player and the leader are left. The leader then tries to mix up this last player and get him to do the wrong thing. As soon as he succeeds in confusing him, the game is over.

HIT THE DUMMY

One player is chosen to be "It" or, as he is called in this game, the Dummy. He stands with his face to the wall at one end of a room, and the others stand about ten feet away from him.

Another player now throws a bean bag or a pillow at the Dummy. As soon as the Dummy is hit he turns around and tries to guess who hit him by examining the expressions on the other players' faces. If he guesses correctly, that person becomes the Dummy. If not, he must be the Dummy again.

KICK FOR THE CORNER

Each player removes his right shoe. Then each player in turn puts his shoe between two books placed on the floor and kicks the shoe toward a corner of the room. The books should be about ten feet from the corner.

The player whose shoe lands closest to the corner is the winner. If one shoe stands on end in the corner it is considered to be closer than a shoe that is lying flat in the corner. If there is a tie, the two players each take an extra kick.

PASS THE POTATO

All the players kneel on the floor in a circle. All but one of them has a potato under his right hand. Someone starts to play a tune on the piano or puts on a record, and while the music is playing, everybody keeps passing potatoes quickly to the left.

The object of the game is to have a potato in your hand when the music stops. The player who doesn't have one is eliminated, and also one potato is taken away. This happens every time the music is stopped, so that there is always one player without a potato. The game can keep on until only one player is left.

LAUGH AND DON'T LAUGH

Play this game fast and you'll enjoy it!

The players sit on the floor in a circle. One player sits in the middle and flips a coin. When the coin lands on the floor he calls out "Heads" or "Tails," whichever it is.

When the coin turns up heads, the players must burst out laughing as hard as they can. But as soon as the player in the middle picks up the coin, they must instantly stop laughing and look very serious.

When the coin turns up tails, the players stay serious, and there is dead silence. No one is allowed to talk. The player in the middle picks up the coin at once and flips it again, hoping that it will come down heads, so that everyone will have a chance to laugh again.

WHO'S THE LEADER?

This is an unusual kind of a game that keeps everybody on his toes every minute.

One player is chosen to be "It" and leaves the room. While he is out, the rest of the players select a leader. The players then stand in a circle and start to clap their hands, and "It" is called back into the room.

He steps into the center of the circle and tries to find out who is leading the others in their actions.

The leader changes from clapping, for example, to stamping his feet, patting his head, jumping up and down or hopping on one foot. All the others do the same thing immediately. They try not to watch the leader too closely, so as not to give him away. It is surprising how quickly the new actions can be followed and how difficult it sometimes is for "It" to locate the leader.

When the leader is discovered, he becomes "It" for the next game.

LAUGH

Almost anything goes in "Laugh." One player volunteers to be "It," and goes to the center of a circle formed by the others. He then tries to make the others laugh or smile by making comical remarks, making funny faces, asking absurd questions, or by doing anything ridiculous he can think of. He can work on one person or on several.

It takes a natural-born comic to be a good "It" in this game, and that is why "It" is a volunteer, instead of being chosen. In almost every group there are several people who would make good "Its" for this

34

game. As players laugh or smile, they join "It" in the center of the circle and try to make the others laugh.

The game goes on until only one player is left outside of the circle. He is called "Gloomy Gus."

ACTING ADVERBS

This old favorite involves some simple acting.

One player is chosen to be "It." He leaves the room, while the others choose an adverb such as "dreamily," "gracefully," or "furiously."

"It" is called in and tries to discover the word by asking players to do different things "in the manner of the adverb." He may, for example, ask the others to eat, walk, dance, read or anything else. Each player then does his best to do the requested action "dreamily" or according to the adverb that was chosen.

If "It" can't guess the word after asking everybody to do something, he can remain "It" for another word, or a new "It" can be chosen. When "It" guesses the word, the last player to act it out for him becomes "It."

"It" doesn't always have to guess the exact word. If he guesses a synonym, it is acceptable. Thus, for "furiously," he might guess "angrily," and that would be counted as a correct guess.

35

JACOB AND RACHEL

A boy is chosen to be Jacob, and a girl to be Rachel. The boy is blindfolded, and both he and the girl are put in the center of a circle formed by the others. Jacob starts by calling, "Rachel, where are you?" Rachel must answer at once, "Here I am, Jacob." She then runs or tiptoes to some other part of the circle to try to avoid being captured. Jacob can call as often as he wishes to, and Rachel must always answer at once. In the end, Jacob captures Rachel by touching her with both hands at once.

After Rachel has been caught, she may be the next Jacob, or else a new Jacob and Rachel can be chosen.

Sometimes, both Jacob and Rachel are blindfolded. This is a good variation, and worth trying out. It means that the two blindfolded players will bump into a lot of people!

MIXED-UP FEATURES

The players sit or stand in a circle with "It" in the center. "It" approaches one of the players, touches his own nose (for example), and says, "This is my ear." The other player must then answer in reverse, by touching his ear and saying, "This is my nose."

"It" counts up to five, and if the player does not answer correctly in that time, he becomes "It."

The new "It" may say, "This is my eye," and touch any other part of his face or body. The game keeps on until everybody has been "It" or until you want to change to something else.

GOING TO JERUSALEM

You set the stage for "Going to Jerusalem" by making a row of chairs, alternately facing one way and the other. There should be one less chair than there are players.

Someone starts a phonograph record, plays a march on the piano, or calls out "Start marching." All the players march around the chairs. Suddenly the music stops or the leader calls out, "All stop." Everyone tries to sit on a chair. There is a mad scramble, and one player will end up without a chair and have to drop out.

Now, one chair is removed from the end of the line and the game goes on. There is another scramble and another player is left without a chair. Then another chair is taken away. At the end, two players march around a single chair until one of them succeeds in getting into it.

STOOP

The boys and girls are paired off as partners, perhaps by playing an Icebreaker such as "Cinderella's Slipper" or "Fishing." Then the players form a double circle, with the boys on the inside and the girls on the outside.

Someone puts on a phonograph record or the leader calls out, "Start marching." The girls then walk in time to the music in a clockwise direction, and the boys walk counter-clockwise.

When the music is suddenly stopped or the leader shouts, "Stop marching," the partners dash to find each other. They take each other's hands and at once stoop down. The last couple to find each other and stoop is out of the game, and the game goes on until only one couple is left or until the guests want to stop and do something else.

HOW DO YOU LIKE YOUR NEIGHBORS?

The players sit anywhere in a room. The leader is in the center of the room. Everyone numbers off, and each person must be sure to remember his number.

"It" now asks some player, "How do you like your

neighbors?" The player can make either one of two replies. He can say, "Very well," and in that case all the players immediately jump to their feet and change seats with their neighbors. In the scramble, the leader tries to get a seat for himself. If he succeeds, the player left without a seat becomes the questioner.

The player may, however, choose the second answer, which is, "I don't like my neighbors." The leader then asks, "Whom would you rather have?" The player answers, for example, "Number Three and Number Eight." These two players must then change seats immediately with the players sitting on each side of the player who called their numbers. The leader tries to get one of the seats left empty during the switch. If he succeeds, the player left without a seat takes the center position and asks the questions.

CAT AND MOUSE

"Cat and Mouse" has plenty of action and gives everyone a chance to join in at the same time.

One player is chosen to be the Cat, and another to be the Mouse. The others form a circle and hold hands. The Mouse goes inside the circle, and the Cat prowls around the outside.

The Cat must try to break through the circle and

catch the Mouse; but the players in the circle do all they can to keep him out by raising or lowering their arms or standing close together. Despite all their efforts, the Cat usually succeeds in ducking under their arms or forcing two players to let go their hands. Then there is a furious chase around the inside of the circle.

You can vary the game by allowing the Mouse to run out of the circle when the Cat gets in. The Cat must then follow the Mouse, who runs around the circle and ducks inside and then out again. The players, in this version of the game, are not permitted to try to stop the Cat after he has once succeeded in breaking into the circle.

SPIN THE PLATTER

There are several different ways to play "Spin the Platter," which has been a favorite party game for many years.

1. The players sit in a circle, either on chairs or on the floor. Each player is given a piece of paper with a number written on it. All the numbers are different. "It" stands in the center of the circle, puts a tin pie plate on edge, and spins it. As he spins it, he calls a number.

The player with that number must jump up and try to catch the plate before it stops spinning and falls to the floor. If he succeeds, "It" must spin the platter again and call another number. But if he fails to catch the plate in time, he becomes "It."

2. A good variation of the game is called "Arithmetic Spin the Platter." When you play this way, "It" does not call a player's number directly, but calls it as a simple problem in addition, subtraction, multiplication or division.

Thus, number 8 could be called as: 4 plus 4; 10 minus 2; 4 times 2; or 16 divided by 2. This makes it a little harder for the players to figure out who has been called on, and gives "It" a better chance to win.

3. "It" holds a cane, an umbrella or a stick upright by pressing his forefinger against its top. As he removes his finger, he calls a number. The player having that number must try to catch the cane before it falls to the floor. This gives "It" a good chance to get out of his place since the cane does not take very long to reach the floor.

4. "It" bounces a tennis ball or volleyball about shoulder high as he calls out a number. Before it hits the floor after the rebound, the player with that number must try to catch the ball. The ball may touch the floor only twice before the player has to catch it. If he misses, he becomes "It."

DROP THE HANDKERCHIEF

This game is an old-timer, but it is as popular as ever.

The players form a circle. Then one player is chosen as "It." He walks around outside the circle with a handkerchief in his hand. He drops it quietly behind one of the players and keeps right on walking, trying to get all the way around the circle before the player discovers that the handkerchief is behind him.

If this happens, the player becomes a "dead fish" and has to stand in the center of the circle. But what usually happens is that the player discovers that the handkerchief has been dropped behind him before "It" succeeds in getting all around the circle. Then the player picks up the handkerchief and dashes off after "It." "It" runs and tries to reach the place in the circle left empty by his pursuer. If he does, the other player becomes "It." But if the original "It" is caught, he remains "It" and must try again.

A "dead fish" can rescue himself in two ways. He may snatch the handkerchief from behind some other player before that player sees it. Or a player behind whom the handkerchief has been dropped may toss it into the circle behind a "dead fish." The "dead fish" then picks up the handkerchief quickly and runs after "It."

✓ TOP DOG

"It" is blindfolded and sits on the floor in the center of a circle formed by the other players. Beside him is a handkerchief. One of the players then starts the game by trying to capture the handkerchief without being detected by "It," who is "Top Dog."

"Top Dog" listens carefully, and as soon as he hears a sound he points toward where he thinks the other player is and calls, "Bow Wow." If he points right at the other player, he wins and remains "Top Dog," and other players try to get the handkerchief.

If "Top Dog" points in the wrong direction, the player continues to tiptoe toward him. If he succeeds in getting the handkerchief without being found out, he becomes the new "Top Dog."

HANDKERCHIEF CATCH

One player is "It" and stands in the center of a circle formed by the others. He holds a handkerchief crumpled up in his hand.

"It" throws the handkerchief into the air and, as he does so, calls out the name of someone in the circle. That player must catch the handkerchief before it touches the floor. If he fails to do so, he becomes "It."

SARDINES

One player is sent out of the room to hide. After five minutes the others start out to find him, each player going by himself.

When a player finds the hidden player, he keeps quiet and hides with him. Or if he sees other players nearby, he keeps on pretending to hunt until the coast is clear, and then slips in with the hidden player.

The game keeps on until all the players find the hiding place, in which everybody is packed in like sardines. Closets make good hiding places, since they can hold a lot of people. Other good places are behind doors and sofas and under tables.

PUSSY WANTS A CORNER

All the players except "It," who is "Pussy" in this game, sit on chairs or stand with a hand against a table or some other object that provides them with a "corner." "Pussy" goes around from one player to another, saying, "Pussy wants a corner." But everyone shakes his head and tells him, "Go to the next-door neighbor."

The players watch each other all the time, and any two players may signal each other by a wink or a gesture and run to exchange corners. This goes on all the time, in fact, and "Pussy" does his best to dash into some corner while it is empty. When he does this, the player who is left out in the cold becomes "Pussy."

If "Pussy" finds it too hard to get a corner, he calls out, "Everybody change." Each player must then exchange his corner for another, and in the scramble "Pussy" is pretty certain to find a corner for himself.

WINK

This game never loses its appeal or its excitement at a party when both boys and girls are present.

Arrange in a circle enough chairs for all the girls, plus one extra. A boy stands behind each chair, and all the girls are seated. The boy standing behind the empty chair tries to get a girl to run over and sit in it. He does this by winking. When he winks at a girl, she must immediately try to get out of her chair and dash across to the empty one.

Each boy keeps his hands on the back of the chair in front of him, but he may not touch the girl until she tries to run away. Then he can put his hands on her shoulders, and if he does this quickly enough, the girl must stay put. The winker keeps on trying one girl after another, until one of them succeeds in escaping. Then the boy left behind her empty chair becomes the winker.

DUCKS FLY

The players stand in a line, with one chosen to be the leader standing in front of them. The leader starts off by saying, "Ducks fly," and flapping his arms like wings. All the other players must immediately flap their arms, too.

The leader continues by saying, "Cats meow," and meowing. All the others copy him. Next may come, "Horses trot," "Hens cluck," "Roosters crow," and "Cows moo." Each time everyone makes a sound or the appropriate motions.

46

After a few animals have been named, the leader tries to trick the others. He makes a false statement such as "Roosters cluck" or "Dogs moo," and starts to cluck or moo, as the case may be. If any player starts to cluck or moo after him, he is out of the game and leaves the line. The game can keep on until all the players are out.

CLAP IN, CLAP OUT

You need both boys and girls to play "Clap In, Clap Out," and this makes it a good game for a mixed group. It is a good game to use to pair off couples.

The boys leave the room and number off. The girls stand behind chairs, either in a straight line or a circle.

One of the girls starts the game by calling out a number. The boy who has that number enters the room, and as he enters all the girls clap their hands.

The boy tries to decide from the sound of her voice which girl called him. He sits down in the chair in front of her. If he is wrong, the girls keep right on clapping. The boy tries chairs until he gets the right one. Then the girls stop clapping.

The game goes on until all the boys have been called in and have found the girls who called their numbers.

HUNT THE SLIPPER

This is always a good game for a party.

Everybody sits on the floor in a circle, except the one who is going to be "It." (He is known in this game as the Customer. All the other players are Cobblers or Shoemakers.) One of the girls takes off a shoe.

The Customer gives the shoe to one of the Cobblers and says:

> "Cobbler, cobbler, mend my shoe;
> Get it done by half-past two."

He then turns his back, and the Cobblers pass the slipper around the circle. One of the Cobblers finally keeps it and hides it under his coat or wherever else he can conceal it.

The Cobblers then say, "O.K. Your slipper's mended," and the Customer turns around and looks at everyone, trying to find out who has the slipper. He can look for a short time, and then must turn around again.

He might have a hard time locating the slipper, but it is made easier for him by the fact that the Cobbler who has the slipper must try to pass it to his neighbor. He will do this, of course, when the Customer's back is turned, but the Customer keeps turning around and trying to watch everybody all the time.

48

If the first Cobbler succeeds in passing the slipper unobserved, the one he gives it to must try right away to give it to his neighbor.

When the Customer finally finds the slipper, the Cobbler who has it becomes the Customer for the next game.

EARTH, AIR, FIRE AND WATER

This game combines plenty of action with quick thinking.

The players divide up into two equal rows, each side seated facing the other in chairs or on the floor. A handkerchief is knotted at one corner, so it can be thrown, and is given to any one of the players.

This player throws the handkerchief into the lap of a player on the opposite side. As he throws it, he calls out, "Earth," "Air," "Fire," or "Water."

If he says "Earth," the player in whose lap the handkerchief lands must name an animal.

If he says "Air," the player must name a bird.

If he says "Water," the player must mention a fish.

But if the player calls "Fire," the other player must be absolutely silent. If he says anything at all, he is out of the game.

As soon as the handkerchief lands in someone's

lap, the thrower starts to count rapidly to ten. If a correct answer is not given before ten is reached, the player is eliminated. The game goes on until all the members of one side have gone down.

STAGECOACH

The players sit in a circle, and the leader, or driver of the stagecoach, is in the center. He gives each player the name of some part of a stagecoach. These names can include: wheel, hub, spokes, horses, harness, bridle, bit, brakes, seat, door, baggage, passengers, driver, step, axle, whiffletree and lantern.

The driver tells a story about a stagecoach that makes a journey with a full load of passengers. He makes it as dramatic and full of thrills, spills and hold-ups as he can. As the driver talks he tries to mention all the different parts of the coach. As each part is mentioned, the player representing it must get up and run around his chair.

Suddenly the Driver shouts: "The whole stagecoach turned over!" At this, all the players jump up and run for different seats. The Driver runs for a seat, too, and if he gets one, the player left without a seat becomes the Driver and starts another story about the stagecoach and its perilous trip.

FOX, GUN, MAN

The faster this game is played, the better, for the object is to confuse the players and get them to do the wrong thing.

The players sit in a circle with "It" in the middle. "It" tells the story that goes with the game. He says:

"The fox is the sacred totem animal of the Fox Indians. The only thing superior to the fox is the gun, which can shoot the fox. The only thing superior to the gun is the man, who can fire the gun. The only thing superior to the man is the fox, because he is the sacred totem animal of the Fox Indians."

51

For those who don't know the game he explains that the sign of the fox is made by putting the thumbs to the ears with fingers outstretched. The gun is made by holding the arms as if shooting, and the man by standing up with the hands on the knees.

"It" then stands in front of some player, makes one of the signs, and starts to count ten. The player must make the sign of the person, animal or object immediately superior to it before "It" reaches ten. If he gives the correct sign in time, "It" must try another player. If he gives the wrong sign or doesn't give any sign at all before "It" reaches ten, he then becomes "It."

MUSICAL CLAPS

In this game the players are divided into two teams. Each team secretly chooses a popular tune, which it is certain the other side will know. Then the first team claps to the rhythm of its tune, and the other team tries to guess its name.

If the second team fails to guess the tune, the first team can clap it out again, and once again—three times in all. Then, whether the tune is guessed or not, the second team claps the beat of its tune and the first team tries to identify it.

SIMON SAYS

"Simon Says" is most fun to play when you have eight, ten, or even more players.

The players sit in a semicircle, except for "It," who sits out in front of the others. All the players, including "It," or "Simon," hold their closed fists on their knees, with their thumbs sticking up. (The game can also be played by having the players sit around a table with their fists on it.)

"Simon" starts the game by calling out one of three commands: "Simon says 'Thumbs up,' " "Simon says 'Thumbs down,' " or "Simon says 'Thumbs wigwag.' " "Simon" suits his actions to his commands, and the players do the same. They either keep their thumbs up, turn their fists so the thumbs point down, or hold the thumbs up and move them sideways to wigwag them.

As long as "Simon" begins each command with the words "Simon says," everything is all right. But if he omits these words and says simply "Thumbs down" or "Thumbs up" or "Wigwag," the players must not carry out the command. They keep their fists just as they are at the time the command is given. "Simon" tries to fool them by making the motion he calls for whether he says "Simon says," or not.

If a player makes a mistake, he becomes "Simon."

POISON PENNY

This is a good game for from ten to fifteen players.

Everybody stands or sits in a circle except the leader. He plays music on a record player or piano, and while the music is playing the others pass a penny to the right around the circle.

When the leader stops the music, which he does frequently, the player who is caught holding the penny is "poisoned." This means that the next time the penny comes around to him, he has to pass it under his left leg, lifting his foot up in the air. If he is unlucky enough to be poisoned a second time, he must pass the penny under both his left leg and his right leg before giving it to the next player.

After this, he can be required to pass it beneath both legs, then in back of his waist, over his shoulders and neck, under the left arm, and under the right arm.

If you don't have music, the leader can blow a whistle, clap his hands or call out "Stop!" as a signal for the players to stop passing the penny.

POSTMAN

"Postman" calls for from ten to fifteen players. It is a chair-changing game.

The players sit in a circle with one player in the center. He is the Postman. Every other player is given the name of a city, which he must be sure to remember.

The Postman starts the game by saying something like: "I have a letter going from Denver to Pasadena." The two players who were assigned these two cities must jump up and try to change seats. But the Postman is on his toes, too, and does his best to get one of the empty seats. The player who fails to get a seat is the next Postman.

FARMYARD

This is a wonderful game, and a very noisy one, for a party where there are from fifteen to thirty people.

The host writes the names of different animals on slips of paper and gives one slip to each guest. Depending on the number of guests, he may write the name of the same animal on from three to five slips.

If there are fifteen guests, for example, it is a good idea to use the names of five animals—duck, dog, cat, sheep and pig, for example. Write "duck" on three slips of paper, "dog" on three slips, and so on.

When everyone has received his slip of paper and

knows what animal he is, all the players are blind-folded. Then, at a signal, the players start imitating the animals of their slips in order to attract the others who have drawn the same animal. They try to find each other.

When two dogs, for example, find each other, they hold hands and hunt for the one or more other players who are barking like dogs. The first group to get all its members together wins; but the game usually keeps on until all the animals have got together in their own groups.

CHARADES

Charades are a never-ending source of interest. If you play Charades just once you'll see its tremendous possibilities for entertainment.

Usually the players divide into two teams. One team chooses a word and different members of the team—either singly or in pairs or groups—act out the various syllables that make up the word. The other team tries to guess the word that is acted out. Then the next group enacts a word of its own.

For example, a two-syllable word that would be simple to act out is "background." One player could scratch his back or another player's back to indicate the first syllable, and another player could pat the ground and lie down on it to give hints about the second syllable.

To do "rainbow," one player might pretend to walk through a rainstorm with a real or imaginary umbrella, while a second player could pretend to shoot something with a bow and arrows.

Most of the time people play this game in pantomime, without speaking. But if it seems necessary, in order to make the meaning clear, you can talk. And when you become a real charades fan you'll act out unusual words, popular phrases and even old proverbs!

Quiet Indoor Games

Bookworms and Strong Silent types will find these quiet games just as much fun as will the life of the party. They call for keen wits, quick reactions, and a crew of solid-senders who come up with the right responses in split-second time. And because they're called "quiet," don't think they're dull. They just don't involve as much running around as the active games do.

Use these fairly early in the evening at your next party, and save some of the more unrestrained games for later on. Everyone will enjoy the thrill of a friendly Battle of Wits. Stage a Battle of the Sexes to see which is really on the beam. Any number of boys and girls can have a dilly of a time with these!

DOWN YOU GO

This is one of the best of the newer games. It has often been played on television.

A leader is chosen, and he thinks of a phrase of three or four words. He might choose, for example, "salt and pepper" or "love is blind." He then makes dashes on a large piece of paper, one dash for each letter in the words he has chosen.

Now it is up to the other players to guess the words. The leader always gives them a hint. For "love is blind" he might say, "This is a proverb." For "salt and pepper," "These go with food."

The players call out letters one at a time. If a letter belongs in one of the words, the leader writes it down over the correct dash. If a player calls a letter that is not contained in the phrase, the leader cries, "Down you go!" and the unlucky player is out of the game.

Set a time limit of five minutes or so to keep the action going. And here's a hint: Call out the vowels first. (They're a great help in guessing the words.)

You can play this game just for the fun of it, or you can keep a score of the correct letters called out by each player. The winner is the person who first guesses the complete phrase. If no one does this within the allotted time, whoever guessed the greatest number of letters correctly is the winner.

ELECTRIC CURRENT

Everybody stands in a circle, holding hands. "It" is in the center of the circle. He is told to close his eyes for a few seconds while a player is chosen by pointing or nodding to start the electric current going around the circle.

The current is started by the chosen player, who squeezes the hand of the player at his right. That player must at once squeeze the hand of the person at *his* right, and the current must be kept going in this way continuously.

The players in the circle try to keep "It" from seeing where the current is. But "It" watches closely and sooner or later will see someone pressing his neighbor's hand. He points to him at once. Then the player who has been caught becomes "It."

BACKWARD SPELLING

Write down a list of common words that contain from six to eight letters. For example, words like "common," "contain," "letters," and "example"! Then have a spelling bee in which each player has to spell a word *backward*.

It takes quick thinking and is not as easy as you

might think. A lot of players are likely to get hopelessly confused, particularly if the game is played fast.

AROUND THE CIRCLE

In this game someone is pretty sure to get the giggles very quickly. Before long almost everybody will be howling with laughter.

The players sit in a circle close together on the floor. Then one player starts the game by turning to the person on his right and doing something to him. He may tickle him in the ribs, tickle him under the chin, pat the top of his head, pat his cheeks, pull his nose, pull his ear, muss up his hair a little, or anything else that occurs to him.

Whatever the first player does must be copied, in turn, by all the other players. No one is supposed to laugh or smile or make a sound of any kind. But the silence usually doesn't last very long!

DETECTIVES

Three players are chosen to be detectives, and are sent out of the room. The others then select an object which the detectives are to try to discover.

The object may be a piece of furniture, a book in a bookcase, a button on someone's coat, or anything else.

The detectives are called in and set out to solve the mystery by asking questions. They can ask each of the other players three questions only. They are not allowed to ask a player if the object is on his own person; but they may ask him if the object is on some other person.

The detectives can usually locate the object by clever questioning. The best idea is to try first to discover its location. Then it is usually fairly easy to find the specific object in that location.

THE WORD GAME

This is a very absorbing game, and a good one to play when there are ten or more players.

Each player is given a narrow strip of paper cut lengthwise from a pad, and is told to write his name on it. Then everybody is told to write a letter of the alphabet—any letter at all—near the left end of his paper. The papers are then folded over to hide the letters, and are passed to the next player.

He adds a letter, which must be a vowel. Then the papers are passed on again. This keeps up until each player has written a letter on each strip of paper. At the second, fifth and seventh passes, players should be told to write vowels.

The strips are then unfolded by the people whose names are on them, and they make the letters into as many words as they can.

Suppose you have the strip shown here. You will see that you can arrange the letters to make the words In, On, Sin, Out, Bun, Bet, Bin and Editor. Look harder and you will find still other words to make.

B U F D T E O R S I N

in   sin   bun   bin
on   out   bet   editor

The scoring is as follows: two-letter words count 5; three-letter words, 8. Four-letter words count 15; five-letter words, 25; six-letter words, 50; and words of more than six letters, 100. The player with the highest score, or the first player to make 500, wins the game.

BEAN QUESTIONS

This is an especially good game for fifteen to twenty players.

Each player is given ten beans. Then they all walk around the room, talking and asking each other questions. Each player tries to trick the others into answering yes or no. Whenever someone says yes or no in his answer, he must give a bean to the player who asked him the question. The player who has the largest number of beans at the end of ten minutes is the winner.

The questions are not hard to think up. For example, "Your name is Bob Beacham, isn't it?" "Swell party, isn't it?" "I'm having a good time here, aren't you?"

Players can answer "Uh-huh" or "Perhaps" or "I think so." But sooner or later they will forget and say yes or no. And this all adds up to quite a hill of beans!

MOTHER GOOSE QUIZ

Just about everybody has been brought up on Mother Goose rhymes, and that's why this game has such a great appeal.

One player starts by asking a question about a Mother Goose rhyme or character. For example, he asks, "Who was told to blow his horn?" The first player to call out "Little Boy Blue" is the winner.

He must recite the rhyme, and then may ask the next question. If he isn't able to recite the rhyme, some other player is allowed to do so. That player then asks the next question: "Who lived in a shoe?" "Who stole a pig?" "Who grew cockleshells?"

WHO HAS THE PENNY?

This old favorite calls for a little skill on the part of "It," who has to try to fool the other players.

The players sit in a circle, holding their hands in front of them with their palms together and their thumbs up. "It" stands in the center, holding a penny between the palms of his hands, which are pressed together.

"It" approaches each player in turn. He draws his hands between their palms, and leaves the penny between the palms of one of the players. When "It" has completed going around the circle, he points to a player and says, "Penny, penny, who's got the penny?"

The player who has the penny, of course, tries to keep a straight face.

The player has two guesses. If he fails to guess the right person, "It" calls on another player. The player who answers correctly becomes "It."

ANIMALS

This is a game in which the leader tries to catch the players, and the players try to catch the leader.

The leader starts by saying, "I am thinking of an animal whose name begins with M" (or any other letter). Suppose the animal is a mink. The players try in turn to guess the animal by asking indirectly about animals whose names begin with M.

A player may ask, "Does it hang by its tail?" The leader must answer at once, "No, it isn't a monkey." If the leader fails to guess the animal to which the player refers, he loses, and someone else is chosen as leader.

If the leader guesses correctly, the next player may say, "Is it very stubborn?" The leader answers, "No, it isn't a mule." The games goes on until "mink" is guessed, when the leader says, "Yes, it is a mink." If no one succeeds in guessing "mink," the leader starts again with another letter. Otherwise, the player who guesses correctly becomes the leader.

If a player fails to name an animal beginning with the right letter, or names an animal that has already been named, he is given a black mark. After three such marks, he is out of the game.

The game can be played in the same way using birds, flowers, foods or cities.

HOW THEY MET

This game has been popular for a long time and always makes people laugh.

Each player is given paper and pencil and is asked to write the name of a girl at the top of his sheet. The girl may be present or may be someone that everybody present knows. Then each player folds his papers to hide the name he has written and passes it to the player at his left.

Just below the fold, the players now write the word *met* and the name of a boy. This is folded over and the paper is passed to the left again. Next, the players write the place where the girl met the boy, fold the paper and pass it. Following the same folding and passing procedure the players then write:

> The circumstances that brought the boy and girl together.
> When they met.
> What he said to her.
> What she said to him.
> What he did.
> What she did.
> How it ended.
> What the neighbors said about it.

After the papers have been passed for the last time, each player reads out loud the one that he is holding.

THREE BUTTONS

It is luck that decides who wins in this guessing game, which has an unusual twist to it.

There should be four or more players, and each one is given three buttons or three pebbles, matches or other small objects.

At each turn the players have a choice of keeping their right hands empty or putting one or more buttons in them. One of the players says, "Hold your hands out," and all players put their closed right hands out in front. Each player in turn then guesses a number which he feels is *not* the correct total of all the buttons in all the players' hands. A player can guess any number between zero and the total number of buttons being used. If there are four players, for example, there will be a total of twelve buttons.

After each player has made his guess, they all open their hands and the buttons in them are counted. Any player who has guessed the *correct* number drops out, and the game is played once more. Finally, there will be only one player left and he is the winner.

RELAY SPELLING

The players divide into two teams and each team sits in a line, facing the members of the other team. A leader then gives a word to one team. The first player says the first letter, the next player the second letter, the third player the third letter, and so on.

This is a little more difficult than when one player spells the entire word himself, for some player along the line is almost certain to give a wrong letter. When this happens, it scores a point for *the other side*. The next player is then given a chance to call out the correct letter.

Each side must remember which player gives the last letter of a word, because the player next to him

69

will be the one to begin spelling the next word when that side's turn comes again.

The teams take turns at spelling words. The team with the highest score wins.

TAKING A TRIP

The players are seated around the room and one of them starts the game by saying, "I am going on a trip and will take an armchair with me," or anything else that begins with the letter A. The player on his right repeats what he has said and adds something that begins with B—for example, a book. Then the next player repeats what the first two have said and adds a word that begins with C, like cabbage.

This goes on as long as each player can remember and repeat what each person before him has said. A point is scored against the players who do not repeat correctly, or who can't think of something beginning with their letter.

A very good variation of this game is to play it the same way, but use the names of cities. For example, "I am going on a trip and will visit Annapolis." The next person might say, "I am going on a trip and will visit Annapolis and Boston." Foreign cities can be used as well as those in the United States.

WORD EXPERTS

Don't move the chairs and sofas to play this game —everyone can sit where he likes in the room. "It," as usual, sits or stands in the center. He points to someone, calls out a letter, and starts to count to ten. Before he reaches ten the player he is pointing at must say a word that starts with the given letter.

"It" can count as fast as he wishes to, and some player is bound to be unable to think of a word in time. When this happens, the player who fails becomes "It."

I AM GOING TO WASHINGTON

The players sit anywhere in a room, and one of them starts the game by pointing at another player and saying, "I am going to Washington." Immediately he starts to count to ten and before he reaches that number, the other player must call out the name of something that begins with W, such as washing machine or watch.

If the other player succeeds in naming something correctly, he points at another player and says, "I am going to Kansas City" or some other city, state or country. If a player fails to supply a word beginning with K, before the first player counts to ten, he is out and the first player continues by pointing to another player and saying that he is going to some other city.

If you find that this is easy for your group, you can have each player name two things beginning with the first letter of the city. And, if you want to make it really hard, you can ask each player to name three things!

OUR COOK DOESN'T LIKE PEAS

Two or three of the players should know the secret of this game ahead of time. One of them starts by saying, "Our cook doesn't like peas, but she likes beans." Another one will say, "Our cook likes cabbage, but she doesn't like green peppers."

The players who are in the know keep on telling about this mysterious cook, and it is up to the rest of the players to try to figure out why she likes some things and not others. As each one catches on, he joins the conversation with more of the cook's likes and dislikes. "She likes radishes, but doesn't like peaches." "She likes lobster, but not pineapples." The secret is that she doesn't like anything that begins with the letter P.

TILLIE WILLIAMS

This game works on the same principle as "Our Cook Doesn't Like Peas," but may be a little harder for some people to catch on to.

Two players who know the secret start the game by talking about Tillie Williams. As other players catch on, they join in the mystifying conversation about this strange character. You can tell if a player has guessed the secret by the way he talks about Tillie.

The first two players might say:

"Tillie Williams is silly, but I don't think she's crazy."

"She's odd, but she isn't really strange."

"She likes coffee, but, oh boy, how she hates tea!"

"She loves floors, but not ceilings."

"They tell me she likes the Mississippi and Missouri rivers, but can't stand the Hudson or Ohio."

"She likes to wear slippers, but hates shoes."

Then someone may say, "I think Tillie Williams likes cabbage, but doesn't like cauliflower."

At this, the first two players will say, "That's right," and the player who has caught on joins in the conversation.

Have you caught on yet?

The fact is that Tillie Williams only likes things

that are spelled with double letters in this game.

As the game continues, more and more players will catch on, and it will get funnier and funnier as people think up new things that Tillie likes and doesn't like.

FLOWER QUIZ

Quiz games are always good fun, if they are hard enough but not too hard. Most people can do pretty well with this quiz.

Each player can answer the questions for himself, or the players can be divided into two or more teams. Give the players ten minutes in which to figure out their answers.

The questions should be written or typed on separate pieces of paper ahead of time, and there should be one set of questions for each player. The questions and the correct answers are:

1. What flowers do we all have? Tulips.
2. What do unmarried men often lose? Bachelor's buttons.
3. What did the teacher do when he sat on a tack? Rose.
4. What do many penniless people hope to do? Marigold.
5. What flower is an American pin-up girl?

American Beauty.

6. What flower is like a lot of birds? Phlox.
7. What flower is some stage scenery made of? Shamrocks.
8. What flower is an eyeful? Iris.
9. What flower describes a pretty girl who has had a quarrel with her boy-friend? Blue bell(e).
10. What flower is a dressed-up wild animal? Dandelion.

GOING TO EUROPE

Two or three of the players should know the catch in this game ahead of time. One of them says, "I'm going to Europe next week and I'm taking a barrel." The catch is that he is going to take to Europe something that begins with the first letter of his first name. The first player's name was Bob. He could also have used R for Robert, and take a raincoat with him.

The next person's name is Helen, and she says, "I'm going to Europe next week and I'm going to take a helicopter." Another player must try to understand what the trick is. If he guesses wrong, he is told he can't go to Europe just yet. The game keeps up until everybody catches on.

RHYMING WORDS ✓

You can play this game at any time with either a small or large group.

One player starts by saying a word of one or two syllables. The player at his right must then say a word that rhymes with the first one. The next player must do the same, and so on around the group. A sample might be: Pan-can-ran-tan-fan-man.

Sooner or later a player will not be able to think of a rhyming word. That player has one point scored against him, but he starts another word to start the ball rolling again. When a player has three points scored against him, he is eliminated.

CALLING CITIES

One player calls the name of a city. The next player must call a city whose name begins with the last letter of the first city. For example, the first player might say Albany. The next player might say York. The next calls Kalamazoo, the next Omaha, and so on.

Each player, after calling the name of a city, starts to count slowly to ten, and the next player must call his city before ten is reached. If he fails he is eliminated. A name can be used only once in the game.

The person who stays in the game the longest is the winner.

GHOSTS

The players sit around the room, and one of them starts the game by saying some letter of the alphabet. The next player adds a letter. Each following player must add a letter, but must try not to finish a word.

If a player finishes a word, he becomes a half ghost and no one may speak to him. Any player who does speak to him also becomes a half ghost. The half ghosts may, however, continue talking and playing.

At any point the player whose turn it is may challenge the person who has just said a letter to name the word he has in mind. If the player cannot do so he becomes a half ghost. But if he can, the challenger becomes a half ghost.

When someone finishes a word, the next player starts a new word. When a half ghost finishes another word, he becomes a whole ghost and drops out of the game. But he still may talk and try to get others to talk to him. If any player talks to him, he becomes a whole ghost. The game is kept up until everybody is a whole ghost.

ZOO

Peanuts are hidden around the room beforehand. The players are divided into groups of three or four, and each group is given the name of some animal. A keeper is appointed for each group.

The players then start to hunt for the peanuts. When a player finds one, he must not pick it up. He must stand still and make a noise like the animal his group represents. He keeps on barking or growling or bleating or whatever it may be, until the keeper for his group comes and picks up the peanut and gives it to him. The player that collects the largest number of peanuts wins.

TREE, FLOWER OR BIRD

This game can be played any time you and some of your friends are looking for something to do. It's fun even on a bus or subway.

The players choose a leader, who says, "Tree, flower or bird—tree!" He points to a player, and starts to count.

The player must name a tree before the leader counts to ten. If he fails, he is out of the game. The last player in the game wins.

I LOVE MY LOVE

This is one of the favorite word games. One player starts by saying, "I love my love with an A because she is amiable." Or he may say "admirable," "affectionate," or any other adjective that begins with A. The next player must say, "I love my love with a B because she is bashful." The third uses the letter C, and so on.

When a player cannot think of a word starting with his letter, he must drop out. Some people rule that X and Z can be left out because there are too few words that begin with them.

BUZZ

This one takes quick thinking. One of the players starts off by saying, "One." The others in turn say, "Two," "Three," "Four," "Five" and "Six." But when "Seven" is reached, that player must say "Buzz."

The counting goes on, but each time there is a multiple of seven or any number with seven in it, the player must say "Buzz" instead of the number. Thus, for fourteen, twenty-one, twenty-eight and others that are multiples of seven, and for seventeen, twenty-seven, thirty-seven and others containing the number seven, the players must say "Buzz." If a player fails, he is out of the game.

UP, JENKINS

"Up, Jenkins" is played by two teams, both headed by a captain, who sit opposite each other at a table.

One team has a button or a penny. The members of this team put their hands beneath the table and pass the button back and forth, keeping it in constant motion. Soon the captain of the team commands, "Down, Jenkins," and each of the players slams both his hands, palms down, flat on the table top.

The other team now tries to guess which player has the button under one of his hands. They check with each other to see if anyone heard the noise of the button striking the table. Then the captain of the guessing team points to some player's hand (which he thinks does *not* cover the button) and says, "Up, Jenkins." The player must lift his hand off the table.

The object for the guesser is to try to guess the hand covering the button *last*. If the hand covering the button is raised earlier in the game, the side holding the button scores as many points as there are hands left on the table.

HUCKLE BUCKLE

This is a hiding and finding game.

Half the players leave the room. The others hide some small object, but leave it in plain sight—in a corner, behind a book on the table, or on top of a framed picture.

The players outside are called back in, told what to look for, and begin to hunt. When a player finds the object, he doesn't give away its location, but sits down somewhere and says, "Huckle, buckle, beanstalk." The hunt keeps on until all the players have found the object. Then the player who found it first has the privilege of hiding it for the second game.

HIDDEN WORDS

Each player is given a piece of paper and a pencil. Then a fairly long word is chosen and everybody writes it down. At the word "Go," all the players start to make as many short words as they can by using the letters of the long word. At the end of five minutes, the player who has the largest number of short words is the winner.

Take, for example, the word "entertainments." With its letters you can make the words: tent, enter, sent, at, it, rain, train, rent, name, net, ten, tart, mart, together with a number of others.

BUTTON, BUTTON, WHO'S GOT THE BUTTON?

The players form a circle, with "It" sitting in the center. One player has a button or a penny. He passes it to a player at his side, who passes it on to the next person. All the players keep their hands in motion all the time, just as though they are passing the button or receiving it from the player next to them.

"It" tries to guess who has the button—which is not always easy. When he succeeds, the player who had the button takes his place.

POOR PUSSY

This is an old-timer, but it is still one of the most popular games for a group of boys and girls to play.

The players sit anywhere around the room. One of them is chosen to be "It" and given a pillow. He puts it down in front of a girl, kneels on it and meows like a cat three times. The girl must keep a straight face and not smile or laugh as she pats him on the head and says three times, "Poor Pussy." If she laughs, she must take the pillow and kneel in front of a boy. A player has to keep going about the room until he makes someone laugh.

CATEGORIES

This is undoubtedly one of the most entertaining pencil-and-paper games ever invented.

First everyone agrees on a word containing five or six letters. (Longer ones can be used if you wish.) Each player then makes a diagram on a piece of paper like the one shown here. The number of columns should be equal to the number of letters in the chosen word. The number of rows should equal the number of categories selected.

The most usual categories are animals, flowers,

vegetables, trees, cities and rivers. But there are many others, such as birds, boys' names, girls' names, colleges, musical instruments, sports, writers, poets and famous people.

Suppose the chosen word is GAMES. This is written as shown, one letter at the head of each column. The leader then calls, say, "Animals," and each player fills in as many columns as he can with the names of animals, each name beginning with the letter at the top of the column.

A player scores one point for each name he writes down, plus one point for each player who did not use the same name. For this reason, it is much better to choose unfamiliar words if you can think of them. The player with the highest score wins the game.

	G	A	M	E	S
animals	Gnu	Anteater	Mule	Elk	Sloth
trees	Gum	Ash	Maple	Elm	Sycamore
cities	Grand Rapids	Ashland	Miami	Eureka	St. Louis
flowers	Gardenia	Arbutus	May apple	Eriogonum	Sun flower

TRAVELERS

A leader is chosen, and he tells the other players that they are all going on a trip. Each player can go to any place he wishes, but when he says what he plans to do there, he may use only words that begin with the first letter of the name of the place to which he is going.

The leader starts the game by asking some player where he is going. The answer may be "Chicago." "What are you going to do there?" asks the leader. "Catch celluloid crabs," would be one of many possible answers. Others could be, "Count crazy change," or "Create cracker candies."

The answers may contain either two or three words, and players are given a reasonable time in which to think them up.

DUMB CRAMBO

The players divide up into two sides. One side leaves the room, while the members of the second side choose a word that can be acted out, such as "sew." The first side is called back and is told that the chosen word rhymes with "go."

It is then up to the first side to try to guess the

word. They make a list of possible words, such as "row," "tow," and "mow." Then they proceed to act these out by making the approximate motions. When they finally hit on the right word, they are loudly applauded by the second side.

The second side then leaves the room and the game is repeated. The side that guesses its word correctly with the fewest attempts is the one that wins.

YOU HAVE A FACE

One player is chosen to be the leader, and all the players sit in a circle. The leader selects a letter of the alphabet to be used in the game, turns to the player on his right and says, "You have a face." The player answers, "What kind of a face?" The leader has said that all answers must be made with words beginning with, say, the letter F, and that no word, once used, may be used again.

The leader may answer, "A funny face." The player then turns to the person on his right, who may say, "A fancy face." Then others in turn have to say, "A fat face," "A friendly face," and so on around the circle. Then the game is played over again using another letter.

Sometimes it's fun to see if you can go around the circle twice with the same letter.

REVERSE

This is a good game to play when there is a brief lull between activities at a party.

The host stands in front of some of the guests and says, "Now listen carefully. Hold your left ear with your right hand, and hold your nose with your left hand." When everyone has done this, the host calls out, "Reverse!" Any player who fails to switch his hands quickly is out of the game. The game can go on until there is only one player left and he, of course, is the winner.

The game can be varied by having the players pat the tops of their heads with their right hands and rub their stomachs with their left hands. When "Reverse!" is called out, they are to pat their heads with their left hands and rub their stomachs with their right hands.

SCRAMBLED FLOWERS, FRUITS AND TREES

Each player is given a list of "scrambled" flowers, fruits and trees. In this list the letters in the names of each flower, fruit or tree have been rearranged to make different words. It is up to the players to unscramble the words and find out what they represent. Give the players ten or fifteen minutes to finish.

Here are some samples you can use. You can work out others if you wish to.

1. Go near. (Orange)
2. He paces. (Peaches)
3. Ah, Lida. (Dahlia)
4. Or a tin can. (Carnation)
5. I'd say. (Daisy)
6. Read Noel. (Oleander)
7. A long aim. (Magnolia)
8. O my cares. (Sycamore)
9. Bees rise or go. (Gooseberries)
10. I love. (Olive)
11. Old man. (Almond)
12. Many a hog. (Mahogany)

LIST THE STATES

While this is one of the simplest games you could think of, the results never fail to astonish the players.

Each player is given pencil and paper. At the word "Go" everyone starts to write the names of the different states. The object is to list all forty-eight in five minutes. It is harder than you might think, and there are usually only a few players who can do it.

TEAKETTLE

To get ready for this wonderful game, it is a good idea to make a list of words that sound alike but have different meanings.

Some examples of words like this are: write—right; rain—reign; in—inn; sore—soar; piece—peace; bare—bear; sow—sew; dear—deer; fare—fair; by—buy; plane—plain; and pair—pear.

To start the game, one player leaves the room and the rest decide on a pair of these words. The player is then called in, and everyone has a turn at saying a sentence that contains the chosen words. But instead of saying the words, you substitute the word "tea-kettle" for them.

Suppose the group chooses "plane—plain." The sentences might then go like this:

"Sue is so teakettle, but she sure knows how to tea-kettle a piece of wood."

"I had the nicest trip in that teakettle."

"Did you ever see one of the big teakettles out West, that it took the pioneers weeks to cross?"

"I think it's his teakettle duty to do the right thing."

The guesser should be given at most five guesses to try to identify the words. If he fails, he is told the answer, and another player goes out of the room.

If you like, two people can leave the room at the

same time. When they come back in, they take turns guessing, and each has five guesses.

PEANUT JACKSTRAWS

The players sit around a table, or at several small tables, and each one is given a drinking glass filled with unshelled peanuts. Each player turns his glass upside down on the table, and then lifts it slowly so as to leave the peanuts in a close-packed pile.

Each player next sees how many peanuts he can remove from the pile without moving any of those left in the pile. The players pick up the peanuts with their fingers. When a peanut in the pile moves, the player has to stop.

The players score ten points for each peanut they are able to remove, and prizes can be given to the three players who make the highest scores.

MY SHIP

This can be played with five players or more.

The players sit around the room, and one starts things going by saying, "My ship is loaded with antelopes," or something else that begins with the letter

A. The next player says, "My ship is loaded with buns," or something beginning with the letter B. Each player in turn tells what his ship is loaded with, using a word beginning with the next letter of the alphabet.

When a player can't think of a word beginning with his letter, he has a mark scored against him. Any player who has three marks scored against him is out. Players must tell what their ships are loaded with in a reasonable time.

Boisterous Games

THESE GAMES are more than usually active or noisy. They are wonderful to play when a group is in high spirits, or when a party quiets down and needs a little new excitement.

Some of these games involve a good deal of rushing and dashing about. Others call for making a lot of noise. Many of them are real "roof-raisers," in which just about anything goes! They are all good fun. Try them, and you will see.

HOT POTATO

This is a game that can be wildly exciting. The players sit in a circle, and "It" stands in the center. The players have a crumpled-up handkerchief, which is the "Hot Potato." They toss it to each other, often pretending to throw and then holding it back in order to confuse "It." It is up to "It" to catch the handkerchief while it is in the air on the way from one player to another. When "It" succeeds, the last thrower of the handkerchief becomes "It." The passing must be fast and continuous to get the most out of the game.

TAP THE BEAR

The player who is the bear sits on a chair in the center of a circle formed by the other players. Another player, the guard, stands in back of him, at one side, or in front. At all times he must keep one hand on the chair, but he can move all around the chair.

The players try to tap the bear on his knee, shoulder, hand, back or any other spot, without letting the guard touch them. When the guard succeeds in touching a player, the guard takes the bear's place, and another player becomes the guard.

BALLOON BASKETBALL

The baskets for this game are made by two of the players who stand on chairs at each end of the room and hold out their arms with joined hands. The other players form two teams of three or four players each. (Three is better unless you have a very large room.)

A balloon is used for a basketball, and the game is played just like regular basketball. There should be a referee who knows the rules of basketball.

JUMP THE ROPE

This game will have everybody literally jumping up and down with excitement. It requires a fairly large room.

The players stand in a circle, and "It" stands in the center. He has a length of rope or strong string, to one end of which a shoe has been tied. "It" holds the rope near the middle and starts to swing the shoe around in a circle. He slowly lets out the rope until the shoe reaches the other players. Then they must jump over the shoe as it comes to them. If the shoe hits someone he is out, and the game keeps on until everyone has been put out.

95

TABLESPOON FENCING

The players are first divided into pairs. Then each player is given two tablespoons and one orange. He holds one of the spoons in one hand, with the orange balanced on the bowl of the spoon. In his other hand he holds the other spoon, which he uses to parry his opponent's blows and also to try to knock his opponent's orange from his spoon.

Some people like to hold the spoon with the orange on it in their right hand, while others prefer the left hand. Try it both ways, and do what seems best for you.

The couples fence with each other, using their spoons, circling around each other, and each lunging to try to knock the other player's orange off his spoon. You can play the game as long as you like, and each couple can keep score, counting the number of times each one makes a point by knocking off the other one's orange.

PARLOR BOWLING

The bowling pins used for this fast-moving game are five small bottles, such as Coca-Cola bottles. They are set up in a line in the center of the room, and "It" stands beside them. All the other players stand or kneel in a circle around the bottles.

One player starts by throwing or rolling a rubber ball at the bottles. He may or may not hit a bottle. In either case the ball will come within reach of some other player, who immediately throws or rolls the ball at the bottles, trying to hit one. When a bottle is knocked over, "It" must put it back in place at once before another player throws. If he does this, the last person to throw the ball becomes "It." But if "It" isn't quick enough to stand up the bottle or bottles in time, he must remain "It."

ZIP

The noisier you can make this game, the better fun it will be. To play it, one of the players stands in the middle of a circle formed by the others, who sit on the floor. The one in the middle turns round and round, then suddenly points at some player and shouts as loud as he can, "One, two, three, four, five, Zip."

If he points with his left hand, the other player must shout the name of the player on his left side before the pointer has shouted "Zip." If he points with his right hand, the other player must call out the name of the player on his right immediately.

If the second player fails to shout the correct name before the one in the middle calls "Zip," the second player goes to the middle of the circle. There is no scoring. You just play as long as you want to or until your throats get hoarse from shouting.

HAT SWATTING

Each player is given a paper bag to put on his head as a hat. The bags can be folded or rolled at the edges to make them fit tightly. Each player is also given a swatter made from a rolled-up newspaper.

At the signal to start, each player tries to knock off the hat of one or more of the others with his swatter. He also tries to keep his own hat from being knocked off. When a player loses his hat he is out of the game. The swatting keeps going until only one player is left with his hat on his head.

SWAT

This is one of the most boisterous of all games and has plenty of action.

A newspaper is rolled up to make a swatter and is

placed on a chair in the center of a circle formed by the players. "It" picks up the swatter and walks around the outside of the circle. Soon "It" gives one of the players a good swat, and then dashes once completely around the circle with the player running after him. "It" runs through the place left empty by the player and into the center of the circle. He puts the swatter on the chair and runs back to take the player's original place in the circle.

The player picks up the swatter from the chair and tries to swat "It" before he reaches the circle. If he succeeds, "It" remains "It." If he fails, he becomes "It," and the game goes on.

If the swatter falls off the chair, the person who last touched it must replace it before the game can continue.

HOT SEAT

For this fast game the players sit on chairs in a circle. All the chairs are filled except one, and it is the "Hot Seat." "It" stands in the center of the circle. His object is to try to sit down on the empty chair. But it doesn't stay empty—every time "It" tries to sit down, a player on either side of the empty chair moves over to fill it.

Whenever "It" wants to, he may call, "Move over!" Then all the players must move one seat to the right. During the move "It" tries to get into an empty chair, but the players try to get there before he does.

BALLOON FOOTBALL

The players are divided into two teams, and the teams line up on opposite sides of a good-sized table. A balloon is put on the center of the table for the football. Each team tries to blow the balloon off the other team's side of the table. Neither team may touch the balloon. A good plan is for two or three

101

people to put their heads close together and blow all at once.

Another good balloon game can be played by having the teams bat the balloon across the room with their hands. Each team tries to make the balloon touch the wall behind its opponents.

HOT AND COLD

All the players but one are given tin pans and spoons. The one player leaves the room while the rest choose some object that he is to find after his return. As soon as the object has been decided upon, the players start to beat softly on their tin pans. This signals the player outside to come in.

As the player approaches the object he is to find, the group beats more and more loudly on their pans. If he goes away from it, the beating becomes softer. (If there are no neighbors to disturb, you can make as much of a racket as you like!)

The game can also be played by having the group in the room decide on some action for the other player to carry out. This may be to pull down a window shade, pick up a book and read from it, or anything else. The player is guided to the object he is to use by beating the tin pans.

CHAIRS AND NUMBERS

Arrange chairs in two rows facing each other. Then number the chairs—one, two, three and on up—so that each chair has a different number.

The players sit in the chairs, and each player acquires the number of the chair on which he is sitting. The player in chair one starts the game by calling any number except his own. The person who has that number must answer immediately by calling any number except his own.

If he delays more than a second, he must go to chair one, and the other players all move up one chair, taking the number of the new chair. If a player who has the wrong number answers a call, or if a player calls his own number, the same thing happens. He goes to chair one. When the game is played fast, the players find it hard to remember their numbers after a few changes.

BULL IN THE RING

The players form a bull ring by standing in a circle with their hands joined. The bull is in the center and his object is to break out of the ring. He walks around, looking for a good place to break through, makes sudden dashes, gets down on all fours to try to get under the players' hands, or tries one place and then quickly jumps to another to try to take the players there by surprise.

If he breaks out, he runs and the others try to catch him. The player who tags him becomes the next bull.

HOG TYING

Try this game out of doors, and wear old clothes! Play on good, soft ground where tackles and falls won't hurt when you take a tumble.

Each player is given a piece of rope three feet long. The players are divided into two equal teams. At the signal to start, the teams approach each other and every player tries to tie his rope around the ankles of some player of the other team.

Of course, two or more players can gang up on one player on the other team. But his team-mates will come to his rescue, provided they aren't too busy trying to defend themselves. It is a wild scramble and a strenuous game.

The team that ties the greatest number of "hogs" in a given time wins. Usually, the time is ten or fifteen minutes, but it can be much longer if desired, and if everybody is having a good time.

Racing Games

Don't start running. This is no Olympic meet. You don't need a college race track—in fact, these races can be played in or out of doors. It might be wise, though, to move vases and lamps out of harm's way, as well as the coffee table. But don't let any party-prissies back out of these. They're really good! Try them the next time a party gets dull.

BACK TO BACK RACE

Divide the group into teams of two for this race, telling the partners to stand back to back and interlock their arms. At the word "Go" they run—or try to run—the length of the room. Then, without turning around, they run back to the other end. If partners fall down or trip each other up, which can happen quite often, they are disqualified.

Be sure to try this. It will give you an unusual new experience!

DOG RACE

Do you know how a dog moves its feet when it runs? If you do, you are exceptional, for most people don't know.

In this race the contestants are to run just as a dog does. They bend down so that the palms of their hands and the soles of their shoes are flat on the ground. They then advance first, the right hand; second, the left foot; then the left hand; and fourth, the right foot.

At all times during the race the players must keep the palms of their hands and the soles of their shoes flat against the floor.

FOOT AT A TIME RACE

Two or more people can contest at the same time in this amusing race. Each contestant must go the length of the room by putting one foot directly in front of and touching the other foot at each step. At no time may there be any space between the feet. The heel of one foot must be put down at each step so that it touches the toe of the other foot.

The first one to go down the room and back wins.

FEATHER AND KNIFE RACE

For this race put a small table at each end of the room. On one table put two small, fluffy feathers, like the ones used for stuffing pillows. On the other table put two milk bottles.

Two people race at a time. Each one is given a table knife. They must blow their feathers into the air, then catch them on the blades of their knives, carry them across the room on the knives, and blow them from the knives into the milk bottles. If a feather falls from a knife, the player must catch it on the blade. If it falls on a piece of furniture or on the floor, he must blow it into the air again and catch it on the blade of his knife.

SHOE SCRAMBLE RACE

This is a good race indoors, if you have a fairly large room, but it is even better out of doors.

Start by asking everybody to take off his shoes. All the shoes are put in a pile at one end of the race course, and are thoroughly mixed up.

The players divide into teams of four or five people each, and stand at a starting line about 50 feet from the shoes (closer if you are indoors). At the signal to start, the first player of each team runs to the pile, picks out his own shoes, puts them on, and runs back to the starting line. He tags the next player, who repeats the performance, and the race goes on until all the players have finished. The first team to finish wins.

This race can also be run if you have only a few players. In this case all the players race to the pile at the same time, find their own shoes, put them on, and race back to the starting line. The first player to reach the starting line is the winner.

CENTIPEDE RACE

It is best to run this race out-of-doors on soft ground. If you try it on a hard floor, it will be

hard on your knees, and also hard on your hands.

Divide the group into teams of two players each. The players on each team get down on their hands and knees, one behind the other. The one in back then grasps both ankles of his teammate in front of him, so that each pair forms something resembling a centipede.

At a signal, the centipedes move away from the starting line. The course should be about thirty feet long. It is safe to say that no speed records will be broken, for the players have to creep along and will find things very awkward. The main difficulty is to keep from tumbling over as they inch their way forward.

BEAN LIFTING RACE

Bean lifting is an art that calls for a steady hand and considerable skill. Try it out and see how good at it you and your friends are.

All the players sit around a table, or several tables if there is a large number. In front of each player is a plate or saucer containing ten beans, and two round toothpicks. The toothpicks are used to lift the beans from the plate and put them on the table.

When the signal is given to start, everybody picks up his toothpicks and concentrates on the delicate and difficult task of picking up the beans. The race may continue for five or ten minutes, or longer if everybody is enjoying it. The winner is the one who has lifted the largest number of beans from his plate and put them on the table at the end of the time.

DIZZY RACE

Each contestant in this race is told to bend down so he is looking at the floor, to rest his forehead on his hands, and then to walk rapidly around in a small circle five times, without raising his head. When he completes the fifth circle, he must raise his head and immediately try to walk in a straight line across the room. (He must have walked in circles as though he had been resting his forehead on top of a cane. If you have canes, sticks or umbrellas available, you can use them and be sure to get the right results.)

Some people can complete only four circles without getting terribly dizzy. The way contestants stagger and lurch when trying to walk straight makes this one of the funniest of all races.

The first one to go through the required motions and get across the room wins.

INCHWORM RACE

In this race each contestant has to move ahead by imitating an inchworm. Each one gets into position at the starting line by putting his hands on the floor and stretching out his body, keeping his knees unbent and stiff and his body raised off the floor.

111

At the signal to start, each one moves his feet forward as close as possible to his hands. During this, the knees may be bent a little as the feet come close to the hands. Then the hands are moved out in front, and the feet are moved up close to them again. It's a race that is fun to watch and fun to take part in.

PAPER CUTTING RACE

Crepe paper is used for this race. Cut a number of pieces ten feet long and one inch wide. Pin one end of each piece securely to the top of an upholstered chair. Give the other end to each player together with a pair of scissors. All the players race to see who will be first to finish cutting his paper ribbon in two all the way to the pinned end. Lots of times, of course, players will cut too fast and cut the ribbon off at one side. When this happens, they are disqualified.

NECKTIE RACE

It is a good idea to have girls take part in this race as well as boys, since some of the girls may not be very good at tying a necktie!

The players are divided into two teams, and each

team stands in a line facing the other. The first player in each line has a necktie, which he ties around his neck. At the signal to start, he must first shake hands with the next player in line, and then untie the tie and give it to the next player. The second player ties it around his neck, shakes hands with the player behind him, unties the tie and passes it on. The winning team is the one on which the last player in line is the first to tie the tie around his neck.

MATCH BOX RACE

For this race divide the players into two teams. Give one member of each team the wooden cover of a small safety-match box.

The leaders of each team pinch the covers over their noses. Then, at the word "Go," another player on each team tries to press the match box cover on his nose without using his hands. The covers are passed from nose to nose down each line. When the cover has reached the last player on a line, that side wins.

If a cover falls to the floor, the player who dropped it may try twice to pick it up with his nose. If he can't do it, he may pick it up with his hands and put it back on his nose.

STICK JUMPING RACE

If there is enough room, three or four people may compete in this race at one time. Their antics will keep the others laughing throughout the race.

For each player put six sticks, pencils, match folders or other small objects in a line on the floor, spaced about two feet apart. Each player stands at one end of his line. He stands on his right foot and holds his left ankle in his right hand in front of his right leg. At the word "Go," the players start hopping over the sticks. When they have hopped over the last sticks, they must hop over all of them again, this time backwards. Also, they must bend down and pick up each stick after they have hopped over it!

114

LEADING THE BLIND RACE

If you are indoors, put a table near the end of the room opposite the starting and finishing line. If outdoors, the racers should go to a rock, around it, and return to the starting line.

Each team consists of one girl and two boys. Both the boys are blindfolded, and it's up to the girl to lead them over the course. She stands in front of the two boys and stretches her hands in back of her for them to hold onto.

If you want to make things still harder and funnier, you can have all the racers hop over the course on one leg.

ORANGE PASSING RACE

Divide the players into two teams. The player at one end of each line has an orange, which he holds beneath his chin. Without using his hands, the player next to him must get the orange from him and between his own neck and chin, and so on down the line. (The antics of the players are very funny!)

If the orange drops to the floor, the player must pick it up with his neck and chin. The first team to pass the orange to the last player in its line wins.

PENCIL AND LEMON RACE

Divide the players into two teams. Then, at a signal, the first player of each team pushes a lemon across the room with a pencil until it touches the opposite wall. He then picks it up and brings it across the room to the starting line, and the next player takes his turn.

Don't try to push the lemon too fast. This will turn it around and slow you up. Easy does it in this race.

STRAW AND TISSUE PAPER RACE

The players are divided into two teams, and each player is given a straw. The two end players on each team are given a small square of tissue paper. They draw in their breath through the straws and hold the papers against the ends of the straws.

The next player in line moves the tissue paper onto his own straw by breathing in through it. He passes it on to the next player's straw, and so on down the line until the last player on a team has got the tissue paper firmly attached to his straw. If the paper falls to the floor, it must be picked up by putting the end of the straw against it and breathing in.

116

PENCIL AND KNIFE RACE

The players are divided into two teams and a table is placed at each end of the room. Two pencils are placed on one of the tables. The first player on each team is given a table knife. At the signal to start, each must get a pencil on the blade of his knife and carry it to the other table. The next two players then take the knives and carry the pencils back to the first table. The first team to finish wins.

BACK-SIDE-DOWN RACE

This is a really hilarious race in which two or more people can compete at the same time.

Each player first lies on the floor on his back. Then he lifts up his body and supports himself on the soles of his feet and the palms of his hands. At the signal to start, the racers crawl the length of the room, moving in the direction in which their heads are pointing.

117

KANGAROO RACE

This race is strictly for boys!

One player gets down on all fours. Another player gets down on all fours, facing in the opposite direction, wraps his legs around the first player's waist, and grasps his ankles, as shown in the drawing.

Another pair of partners get into this position and the two pairs race the length of the room.

PIE PAN RACE

Divide the players into two teams. The first player of each side is given two pie pans, and he puts them on the floor in front of him. At the signal to start, he picks up one of the pans and moves it forward a foot or two. He then places one foot in the pan, balances on that foot, and picks up the other pan. He puts it down a foot or two ahead of him and puts his free foot in it. Then he balances on that foot, picks up the first pan, moves it ahead, and puts his foot in it again.

Each player races the length of the room or across the room in this way, and the team that finishes first wins.

CRACKER RACE

To put everybody at a party into a really silly mood, get them all in this crazy race at the same time. The more the merrier!

Each person is given four soda crackers or saltines. At the signal to start, everybody eats his crackers as fast as he can. As soon as possible after eating the last cracker, each person must try to whistle "Yankee Doodle." The first one to whistle it all the way through is the winner.

CROSS-LEGGED RACE

This race is funniest when three or four or more people race the length of the room and back again at the same time.

Each contestant must cross his left leg in front of his right leg, and keep it in that position while he races the length of the room. Then he must reverse and cross his right leg in front of his left, and race back to the starting point.

Both feet are kept on the ground at all times. When one leg is crossed in front of the other, the foot is not lifted from the floor.

INDOOR OBSTACLE RACE

A wonderful race for parties—but push the furniture out of the way first!

Each racer carries a book high under his right arm. He is told to go to a table (in the same room or the next room) on which there are pieces of string. Each player must tie a piece of string around his left wrist without dropping the book.

All the players then go to another table on which there are a number of books. Each person has to put a book under his left arm without dropping the first book.

Next they run to another table on which there are pieces of string. Each player has to tie a piece of string around his neck. Then they race back to the starting point.

Anyone who drops a book is out of the race, and the first person who gets back without dropping either of his books is the winner.

WHEELBARROW RACE

For this race one player gets down on all fours and another player then takes hold of his ankles and lifts them up into the air. The first player is then the wheelbarrow. One or more other pairs of players get in the same position and they all race the length of the room or, if outdoors, a distance that has been marked off.

Games for Two People

MOST game books contain games that are meant only for parties or for fairly large groups of people. But there are lots of times when two friends are together and can't think of anything especially interesting to do. The games for two people described in this section should lick this problem once and for all!

PIGMY HIDE AND SEEK

This game can be started on the spur of the moment, and kept up as long as it is enjoyable.

One player starts by imagining that he is a pigmy or dwarf. He then hides himself somewhere in the room, in some place that a very tiny person could get into. He can make himself as small as he wishes—even a half-inch tall or less. Then he can hide in a keyhole, an electric light bulb, somebody's pocket, in a thimble, an envelope, in someone's hair.

The other player tries to find out where the pigmy is hidden by asking him questions. There are no restrictions on the type or number of questions.

MENTAL I SPY

One player thinks of some object in the room—for example, a vase on a table, a book in a bookcase, a picture on the wall, a flower in a vase, a box of matches or a door knob.

The other player tries to find out what it is by asking questions that can be answered by yes and no.

"Is it on that side of the room?" "Is it on the table?" "Is it the picture frame?" It is often surprising how quickly the object can be located.

WHEEL OF FORTUNE

Two people can play this at any time, or a larger group can play it, each player taking his turn.

Draw a circle on a piece of paper and draw eight spokes inside it to divide it into sixteen parts. Between the spokes write numbers, one for each space. Then draw a small circle in the center to represent the hub of a wheel.

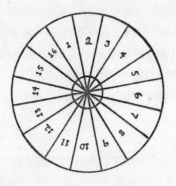

Each player in turn closes his eyes, lifts a pencil from the table into the air and over his head, and brings the pencil point down quickly on the paper. If the pencil point lands in one of the spaces, the number in that space is the player's score. If it lands on a line, or on the hub, or outside the wheel, there is no score.

You can play for twenty-five or fifty points, or for as long as you are having a good time.

TWENTY QUESTIONS

One player thinks of an object anywhere in the world. The other player then tries to guess it by asking not more than twenty questions. The questions must be answered "Yes," "No" or "I don't know."

It is usually a good idea to find out first if the object is animal, vegetable or mineral. This will help to give an idea of its general nature. Then ask if the object is in existence now, if it is in the United States, and so on. Often even the most unlikely objects can be guessed within the limit of twenty questions.

If more than two people are playing, the questioners ask their questions in turn.

HANGMAN

Each player has a pencil and a piece of paper. A category is chosen, such as trees, flowers, birds, cities or rivers. One player thinks of a word in the chosen category and puts down on his paper as many dashes as there are letters in the word.

The other player then tries to guess the word by calling out letters. When he calls a letter that is in the word, the other player must write it over the correct dashes in the word.

When he calls a letter that is not in the word, he must start to "hang himself." He draws a scaffold on his paper with a rope hanging from it. For the first wrong letter he draws a head; for the second a neck; for the third a body, and so on.

If the second player guesses the word, he wins. But if he calls so many wrong letters that the whole figure of the hanged man is completed, he loses.

If more than two people are playing, the players call letters in turn and one hanged man represents all of them.

BATTLESHIPS

This is one of the most fascinating of all games for two players.

Each player has a piece of paper on which he makes

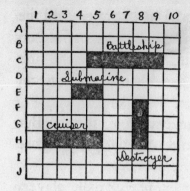
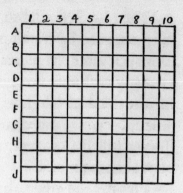

two charts like the ones shown in the drawing. On one he locates his own ships. On the other he keeps a record of the shots he fires at his opponent's ships. Each chart contains a hundred small squares. (Some players use charts that contain a hundred forty-four small squares.)

Each player decides first where he is going to locate his ships on the first chart. He has four ships—a battleship that fills five spaces, a cruiser that fills four spaces, a destroyer that fills three spaces, and a submarine that fills two spaces. The players fill in spaces with their pencils to show where their ships are. They keep their papers hidden from each other.

When all is ready, each player in turn takes a shot at the other player's ships. He does this by calling out the letters and numbers that designate small squares,

127

as D-8, H-4, B-6, and so on. When a player calls one of the squares in which part of one of his opponent's ships is located, he scores a hit.

After each shot is called, the other player must tell if it hit one of his ships, and what ship it was. For example, using the chart shown here, if the other player called C-5, you would have to say, "You hit my battleship."

This lets the other player know that the battleship is near C-5. On his next turn he tries to find out if the battleship is in a vertical or horizontal position. If he thinks it is vertical, he will call D-5 or B-5, and will find out that he is wrong. Then he will know it is horizontal and will call C-4 or C-6.

A ship is sunk when all the squares it occupies have been called out.

As a rule, each player is allowed twenty-five shots for a big square containing 100 small squares, and thirty-six shots for a big square containing 144 small squares. However, you can keep on playing, if you wish, until one player has sunk all of his opponent's ships.

When you call a shot, make a dot in that small square in the second big square on your piece of paper. This will record your misses as well as your hits, and will keep you from calling the same square twice.

BOXES

This game is sometimes called "Dots and Dashes."
To get ready for it, a square is made of thirty-six dots
on a piece of paper—six rows of six dots each. Set the
dots about a quarter of an inch apart. The object of
the game is to make as many boxes as possible by connecting two dots at a time with a line.

The first player starts by connecting any two dots
with a line. The second player does the same. Then
the players continue to draw lines in turn. When one
of them completes a box, he gets another turn, and
after a short while the players are usually able to complete a number of boxes during one turn.

When a box is completed, the player puts his initial
inside it. Then, when the game is finished, each player
counts his boxes, and the one who has the largest
number of boxes wins.

129

HOW MANY WORDS A MINUTE?

Two players can play this game at any time. One of them holds a watch in his hand. When the second hand is at two seconds before the minute, he says, "The letter H. Get going." The other player immediately starts to call out all the words he can think of that begin with the letter H.

The first player carefully counts the words. It is a good idea for him to make a mark on a piece of paper for each word. At the end of a minute he calls "Stop." Then the players change places.

Some letters, of course, are easier than others. (You should leave out Q, X and Z!)

GUESS THE NAME

One player thinks of the name of a famous person and says: "I am thinking of a famous person whose last name begins with M." The other player then tries to discover the name by asking questions about the profession or activities of famous people whose names begin with M. The first player must answer with the name of someone known for that activity. If he fails to do this, the other player can ask some leading question, such as, "Is it a man or a woman?"

For example, suppose that the player is thinking of President Monroe. The other player asks, "Is it a poet?" The first player must say, "No, it isn't Milton."

As the game goes on, the questioner gets to know more and more about the famous person, and in the end usually guesses who it is. The more often the first player fails to give the right answer, the more often the questioner can ask leading questions and get more information.

The game can also be played by a group. One player thinks of a famous person, and the others ask him questions in turn.

STONE, PAPER AND SCISSORS

Two players hold their hands behind their backs. One counts "One-two-three." At "three" they both bring their right hands out in front, holding them in one of three positions.

The first is that of clenched fists, which means stone. Position two means paper—hand open and palm down. The last position is one in which the first and second fingers are extended and the other fingers are closed. It means scissors.

Each player decides, while his hands are behind his back, which position he will use. The scoring is as follows: Stone beats scissors because it makes them dull. Scissors beat paper because they can cut it. Paper beats stone because it can wrap it up.

You can play the game as long as you like, keeping count of the number of times each player wins for the final score.

HUL GUL

This game was invented by the ancient Greeks more than two thousand years ago, and has been played ever since. It is hard to beat.

Each player starts with ten pebbles, beans or other

small objects. One player puts some of his pebbles in his right hand, closes his hand, and holds it out in front of him.

He says, "Hul Gul." The other player says, "Hands full." The first player then says, "How many?" The second player makes a guess as to how many pebbles the first player has in his hand.

If the second player happens to guess the right number, he gets the pebbles in the first player's hand.

If he guesses too many, he must give the first player enough pebbles to make up the number he guessed. For example, if the first player had four pebbles and the second guessed six, the first player would say, "Give me two and make it six."

If the second player guesses too few, he must hand over half of the pebbles he has, up to five. One player is allowed to win no more than five pebbles at a time.

The game continues until one player has won all the pebbles, or until it is a draw and you get tired of playing.

"Hul Gul" can also be played by a number of players. The players are arranged in a circle, and one player starts by holding out his hand to the player on his left and saying, "Hul Gul." After these two have played, the game continues to go around the circle, always to the left. It keeps on until one player has won all the pebbles or until you decide to stop.

PEASE PORRIDGE HOT

"Pease Porridge Hot" is one of those games that have given people amusement for many centuries. We don't know just who made it up, or when. It is included here both because it is fun and because a lot of people aren't sure of the right motions to make when reciting the rhyme.

The two players stand or sit facing each other. Then they recite the following rhyme and go through the motions described below:

"Pease porridge hot,
Pease porridge cold,
Pease porridge in the pot,
Nine days old.
Some like it hot,
Some like it cold,
Some like it in the pot,
Nine days old."

The motions are as follows:

First Line:

Clap both hands to thighs (Pease)
Clap both hands together (porridge)
Clap right hand with partner's (hot)

Second Line:

Repeat first two motions and on the word "cold" clap left hand with partner's

134

Third Line:

Repeat first two motions

Clap right hand with partner's (in)

Clap your own hands together (the pot)

Fourth Line:

Clap left hand with partner's (Nine)

Clap own hands together (days)

Clap both hands with partner's (old)

Last Four Lines:

Repeat the same motions as for the first four lines.

With little practice, you and your partner will be able to go through the motions faster and faster. Then you can show others how to do it.

HINK PINK

"Hink Pink" is a good game for two people. It calls for quickness and imagination. You can play it anywhere, even when walking along the street with a friend.

One player starts by saying, "I have a hink pink." This means that he is thinking of two words of one syllable each that rhyme with one another. For example, fat cat, full bull or big pig.

The player must then add a short description of his

"hink pink." For "full bull" he might say, "My hink pink is a well-fed farm animal." For "big pig" he could say, "My hink pink is a large and greedy farm animal."

Once you begin to play "Hink Pink," you will probably be surprised at how many "hink pinks" you and your friends will be able to think up.

A few more examples would be: wise guys, house mouse, tea tree, green bean, spook book, new glue, old scold, new shoe, peg leg, grand hand and red head.

You can keep score if you want to do so, counting one point against a player each time he fails to guess the other's hink pink. But the main idea is just to have some fun.

ORIENTAL WRESTLING

To wrestle in this way, the two players lie on their backs side by side, with their elbows interlocked and their heads pointing in opposite directions.

Out loud and in unison they count, "One, two, three!" On the first and second counts each brings his leg that is nearest the other player up to a vertical position. At "three" they vigorously lock their inside legs together and each tries to roll the other one up onto his shoulders and then completely over backwards.

Practice can develop your skill to a surprising degree. Many small, wiry players soon reach the point where they can upset other players that are much heavier.

HOP WRESTLING

This is a kind of wrestling you may not have tried.

First, mark a line on the ground. The two players then stand on opposite sides of the line, reaching over it, and grasping each other's hands. Each lifts his left leg, so he is standing on his right foot only. Then they hop and pull, trying to make the other player hop over the line or put down his left foot.

Keep a score of how many times each player succeeds in making the other cross the line or put down his foot. The one with the highest score will then be the winner of the match.

HAND WRESTLING

"Hand Wrestling" can be played at any time, and is sometimes good for an hour or more of fun.

The two contestants stand opposite each other. They put their right feet side by side, and keep their left feet back a little in order to serve as a brace. Then they clasp their right hands, and each tries to overbalance the other by pushing and pulling.

The winner of each bout is the one who makes the other player lift either his right or left foot from the ground.

FINGERS OUT

"Fingers Out" is a game that was invented in China nobody-knows-how-many thousands of years ago.

Two players stand facing each other, and each puts his right hand behind his back. Then they count together out loud, "One, two, three." At "three" they put out their right hands, either closed to make a fist or with one or more fingers outstretched. They can stretch out one finger or two, three or four fingers, or hold their hand open so all five fingers are outstretched.

At the moment they put out their hands, each one shouts a number. This number is his guess as to how many fingers will be outstretched on both hands.

The player who guesses the correct number of fingers or the closest number to it scores a point. The players write down the score, and the winner is the one who has the greatest number of points when it is decided to stop playing.

STEP VOLLEYBALL

This is a good outdoor game for two players, but it can also be played by more than two.

The players use a small hard rubber ball or an old

tennis ball. They stand on a base line marked on the sidewalk in front of the steps of a house. From the base line each player in turn throws the ball against the "risers," or upright sections of the steps.

On the first throw they try to hit the lowest riser. They let the ball bounce back onto the sidewalk and then try to catch it while still standing in back of the base line. On the second throw they try to hit the next highest riser, and so on up to the top step. After hitting the topmost riser, they come down step by step until they reach the bottom.

If a player fails to hit the right riser or fails to catch the ball on the bounce, he loses a turn, and the other player gets two turns in succession. The player who is the first to complete going up and down the steps is the winner.

Stunts

STUNTS at a party are as rousing as a cup of hot chocolate after ice-skating. Wallflowers begin to bloom, and everybody ends by feeling like the life of the party.

These stunts are guaranteed to put everyone taking part in them in a good mood. They're all fun, and some are downright hilarious. You don't have to be a circus performer to do them, and you don't need a large group, either. Try a few of these stunts some rainy afternoon when one or two of the gang drop over, and see if they don't start everyone laughing.

ARTISTIC EFFORTS

Put a footstool or a wooden box in the center of the floor. Each person, in turn, sits on the footstool and holds his left leg straight out in front of him, with the toe pointing upward. He then rests the heel of his right shoe on the toe of his left shoe.

In this position, balancing himself with his left arm, but not touching the floor with his left hand, he tries to write his name on a piece of paper put on the floor at his right. (Reverse this for left-handed people— balance with right arm, put paper at left.)

SPOON LIFTING

For this stunt ask three or four people to kneel on the floor with their knees together. Tell them to bend forward and put their elbows on the floor directly in front of them, touching their knees, with their forearms extended. Their hands must rest on the floor, palms down.

Now put a spoon, right side up, on the floor in front of each person. The handle of the spoon must touch the tip of the player's right-hand ring finger, and the bowl must touch the tip of the ring finger of the left hand.

Everything is now ready. Tell the players to raise their bodies until they are sitting on their heels, and to clasp their hands behind their backs. Then tell them to bend forward and see if they can pick up the spoons between their lips. There's many a slip between spoon and lip, as you will see when you try this!

PAPER SNIFFING

Two people take part in this stunt. To one you give a piece of tissue paper about four inches square and tell him to hold it to his nose by sniffing or breathing in. Then tell someone else to see if he can sniff the paper off the first person's nose just by inhaling. The one who gets or keeps the paper wins.

SIGN YOUR NAME

Fasten a piece of paper to the wall with four thumbtacks. Each player in turn takes a pencil, stands in front of the paper, and starts to swing his left leg clockwise in a circle. When the circle is going full swing, he tries to write his name on the paper. A comical amount of effort must be made to get the pencil under control and to write down the letters.

KNOCK OFF THE COIN

Put a quarter at the edge of a table, with about one-third of the coin projecting over the edge. Each player walks up to the table, holding his right arm straight up over his head. Then, moving very quickly, and not stopping to judge the distance, each player is to see if he can bring his arm straight down and knock the coin off the table with his index finger. His finger must touch only the coin, not the table.

It's surprising how few players can judge the distance correctly.

MILK-BOTTLE EASY CHAIR

This stunt calls for a really good sense of balance, which many people don't have.

Stand a milk bottle upright on the floor and put a book in front of it. Then ask someone to put one foot on the top of the bottle and stand on it, balancing. Then, without touching the floor with his other foot, he is to bend down, pick up the book, regain his upright position on the bottle, open the book and read one or more sentences.

Anyone who succeeds in doing this should be given the grand prize.

144

CHAIR AND CRACKER STUNT

Put a straight-backed kitchen chair on the floor, front legs flat, so that its back is parallel to the floor. Then put a cracker on the top crosspiece of the back. The cracker should rest only partly on the crosspiece, extending a little over the edge on the side nearest the seat of the chair.

Now ask someone to kneel on the crosspiece connecting the back chair legs and hold the chair back close to the seat with both hands. He is then to lean forward and try to pick up the cracker with his teeth. If anyone succeeds, he is more than good—he is expert!

PENNY PLACING

Cut a thin strip of paper and pin it to the floor to make a line, or else use the edge of a rug as a line. Then have each person in turn toe the line and put his left hand behind his back. Put a penny in his right hand, and tell him to put his right hand in back of his right knee, and then move it between his legs. At the same time, he is to bend his knees.

In this position, he is to see how far out in front of him on the floor he can put the penny, without losing his balance. His hand must put the penny squarely on the floor. It must not be dropped. The person who puts the penny the farthest from the line is the winner.

BLINDFOLDED SEARCH

Two or three couples are asked to volunteer for this stunt. Blindfold each person and then turn all of them around and around so they will lose their sense of direction. Then join the hands of each couple and tell them to try to find a book placed on a table near them. They must hold hands at all times, and they are absolutely forbidden to speak to each other.

If any couple let go their hands, they are out of the

game. You will be surprised at what a hard time they will have finding the book, and everybody will laugh at how they try to pull each other in different directions, each one thinking that he knows the way to go.

The first couple to get the book wins.

THUMBLESS STUNTS

Thumbless stunts can keep a party or a group of people amused for a long time. To prepare them, the players are given adhesive tape and help each other to tape their thumbs and forefingers together, making the thumbs on both hands useless.

Here are some stunts you can do:

1. Give each player a box, some wrapping paper, and a piece of string. Each person is to try to wrap up the box and tie the string around it.

2. Untie the shoelaces of each player. At a signal to start, each player must retie his laces. (Not easy!)

3. Give each player an orange and let him try to peel it.

4. Pair off the boys and girls. Give each boy a large handkerchief and tell him to put it around his girl's neck and tie a square knot in it.

The first person to accomplish any of these stunts is the winner.

STRONG MAN STUNT

Tell your friends that you will show them a stunt in which you will prove to be stronger than three of them put together.

When you have three people lined up, give them a broom and tell them to hold it upside down, each with one hand just below the bristles. Put a piece of paper on the floor. Then tell them to hold the broom about one foot above the paper.

Now put your right hand against the broomstick at a point a few inches above its lower end. Tell your friends to see if they can push the stick straight down onto the paper. As they try to do this, you push the stick to one side with your hand, so that it misses the paper.

You can do this easily, because of the leverage you have on the stick. Try it, and you will see.

BROOM JUMPING

This stunt may seem easy to do, but just try it before you make up your mind.

Lay a broom flat on the floor. Then stand one inch behind the broomstick, with both feet together and with the toes of your shoes one inch away from the broomstick. Stoop down, bending your knees, and grasp the stick with the thumb and forefinger of each hand. Your fingers must be on the front side of the broomstick, and your thumbs on the other side. (You should be standing just at the stick's mid-point.)

Now see if you can jump over the broomstick without taking your hands off it, moving the broom, or separating your feet. Your feet must touch each other at all times, and you must not let them touch the broomstick.

There is a secret to success in doing this stunt which may help you a good deal. Use your arms as a pivot and lean as far forward as possible over the broomstick. Raise your toes first, and as you jump, raise your heels.

BROOMSTICK CRAWLING

This stunt will test your agility and muscle control to the limit.

Place a broom upright so that its bristles rest on the floor and touch a wall. Then take the top end of the broomstick in your left hand, and with your right hand grasp the broomstick at a point about one foot below your left hand.

Now, without letting the bristles of the broom move away from the wall, and without letting go of the broomstick, try to crawl behind the broom between your right hand and the floor, and get back to an upright position. It's not easy.

DROPPING CLOTHESPINS

For this stunt, put a milk bottle on the floor just behind a chair. The players must then kneel on the chair, facing its back, take clothespins between their teeth, and try to drop the clothespins into the bottle.

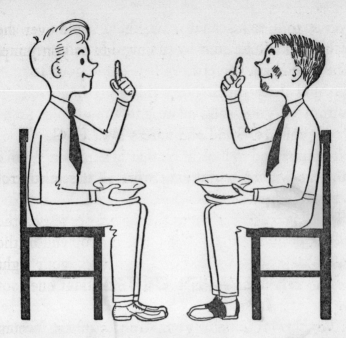

DO AS I DO

Be sure you are a good friend of the person you ask to help you do this stunt.

Blacken the bottom of a soup plate, in advance, by holding it over a lighted candle for a few minutes. Sometime during the party, when people are doing stunts, tell a friend that you don't think he can do exactly what you do for a full minute. If he takes you up on this, go out and bring in two soup plates half-filled with water.

Give him the blackened one, and tell him to keep his

eyes on you, so he can do everything you do without making a mistake. Start by smiling. He will copy you. Then raise your eyebrows, stick out your tongue, and nod three times. Next rub your finger on the bottom of your soup plate and draw your finger across your forehead and across both cheeks. Then tell your friend to look at himself in a mirror. By that time, he will be wondering what all the others are laughing about.

NEWSPAPER CRUMPLING

Try this on some of your strong, athletic friends, and see what happens. They will probably get a big surprise.

Spread out a full four-page sheet of a newspaper. Ask a friend to extend his left arm straight out to the left, at shoulder height. Tell him to turn his left hand so the palm is down. Then put one corner of the newspaper between his left thumb and forefinger and say, "See if you can crumple up all the paper in your left hand."

It is not very easy, but it can be done if you go at it slowly, gathering small sections of the paper at a time into your hand.

CANDY RACE STUNT

A marshmallow or some other candy is tied to the middle of a three-foot piece of strong thread. A boy and a girl stand opposite each other with their hands behind their backs. Put one end of the thread in the girl's mouth, and the other end in the boy's mouth. At the word "Go," the boy and the girl start to chew their way along the thread until one of them reaches the candy. The first one to reach it eats it right away.

PICK UP THE HANDKERCHIEF

Put a handkerchief on the floor, and raise its center up as high as you can. Then call for volunteers for a balancing stunt.

When someone volunteers, tell him to stand facing the handkerchief, about ten inches away. Then tell him to raise his right foot, put it behind his left leg, and grasp his right ankle with his left hand. Now, without losing his balance or touching the floor with his right hand, he is to lower himself, bend forward, and try to pick up the handkerchief with his teeth. If he succeeds, he is to try to stand up straight again, still holding his right ankle with his left hand.

THE BEST COUNTING STUNT

Once you learn this stunt you can have a lot of fun with it. It will almost always fool the friends you try it on. Tell a friend that all he has to do is to name the numbers that are next higher than the numbers you call out. You can tell him that you think it will be impossible for him to name the right number in every case.

You begin with a small number; say, seven. He must immediately reply, "Eight." Then you call a two digit number; for instance, fifteen. He must say, "Sixteen."

You continue with a three-figure number—one hundred fifty-nine, for example. He must say, "One hundred sixty." Go on to a four-figure number such as one thousand, two hundred forty-three. He must say, "One thousand, two hundred forty-four."

Next you call a higher number of four digits, such as three thousand, five hundred and ten. He must say, "Three thousand, five hundred and eleven." Then you say, very quickly, "Four thousand and ninety-nine." Nine times out of ten the other person will say, "Five thousand." (The right number is four thousand, one hundred.)

POTATO BALANCE

Spread a handkerchief on the floor, and raise up its center as high as you can. Then ask someone to stand close to the handkerchief. When he has done so, put on his head a pie pan with a potato in its center.

The player must try to stoop down and pick up the handkerchief with his right hand, without letting the pie pan or the potato drop to the floor. If he succeeds in picking up the handkerchief, he is to try to stand up straight again.

KICK THE MATCH BOX

This is an amusing stunt that you can try at any time.

Tell a friend to stand with his feet together. Then set an empty safety-match box on end directly in front of him, touching the toe of his right shoe. Pull the drawer of the box halfway out.

The player is to step back from the match box, putting his left foot in back of his right foot, then his right foot in back of his left foot, and his left foot again behind his right foot. Then he is to bring his right foot alongside of his left foot.

Now tell him to try to kick over the match box with his right foot. He is not allowed to move his left foot, but he may bend his left knee and bend his waist. Try this yourself, and you will see that it's not too easy.

HYPNOTISM

Tell a friend that you can prevent him from getting out of a chair just by touching him lightly with one finger. The chances are, of course, that he won't believe you.

When he agrees to try the stunt, tell him to sit in

a chair, fold his arms, and stretch his legs out in front of him. You then stand in back of the chair and tell him to look at your face. To do this, he will have to rest his neck on the back of the chair and throw his head far back.

As he looks up at you in this position, put a finger lightly on the center of his forehead and say: "You can't get up." Just as long as you keep your finger on his forehead, it will be impossible for him to get up from the chair.

PARALYSIS

This stunt seems impossible, but you can make it work every time. Tell a friend that you can stand him beside the wall of the room in such a way that he will be absolutely unable to move his right leg. It will be *impossible* for him to move his leg an inch in any direction.

When your unbelieving friend agrees to follow your instructions, tell him to stand against the wall of the room so that his left foot touches the wall, his left hip touches the wall, and his left shoulder touches the wall. Then tell him to try to move his right leg. As long as his left foot, hip and shoulder touch the wall, he will not be able to move his right leg.

MIRROR DRAWING

Sit a player at a table and, in front of him, stand a book with the covers partly opened. Directly behind the book, on the side away from the person, lay a piece of writing paper. Just back of the paper stand a mirror, so that when the player looks over the book into the mirror, he can see the paper in the mirror, but can't see the actual paper.

Now give the person a pencil. Tell him to put his hand around the right end of the book and put the point of the pencil near the center of the paper. Then tell him to draw a square on the paper while looking into the mirror. After that, he is to draw two diagonals across the square.

When players try this for the first time they seem to have no control over the pencil and draw the most peculiar designs!

SIAMESE SIT DOWN

Two boys stand back to back, with their heels and heads touching, and their arms folded across their chests. They then try to lower themselves to a sitting position on the floor by bending their knees and moving their feet slowly out in front of them. But their

shoulders and heads must always touch each other, and they must keep their arms folded. They must try to sit down on the floor with their legs extended in front of them.

If they succeed in this, they must try to stand up again, following the same rules as on the trip down. The getting down is fairly easy, but the getting up is terrific!

LIFTING A PERSON WITH FIVE FINGERS

This is a surprising stunt, which works well if you follow carefully the directions given here.

Someone sits in a straight-back chair with his hands clasped in his lap. Then five other players gather around the chair. Two players stand at each side of the chair, and the fifth person stands behind the chair.

The two players nearest to the front of the chair now put their right forefingers under the knees of the person in the chair. The two others at either side put their forefingers under his armpits. The player in back puts his forefinger under the sitter's chin.

Tell the person in the chair to keep his head rigid and slightly bent forward. Then announce that when you count to three, the five people whose fingers are touching the person in the chair must take a deep breath and raise their fingers all at once. When this is done, the person in the chair will suddenly rise into the air as though he were light as a feather!

Outdoor Games

Who says you're too busy for "Cross Tag" or "Duck on a Rock"? You're never too old for an afternoon in the great outdoors, running, hiding, chasing, dodging until you're out of breath and laughing hard.

Organize a hiking party or a picnic someday soon and shake the cobwebs out of your head. Confirmed armchair warmers will be the first to blow off steam and enjoy the games in this section. Some of these are old favorites that just had to be included, they're so good. Others will be new to you and your friends.

SNATCH

The players are divided into two teams of equal size. Two lines are marked on the ground about thirty feet apart, and each team stands behind its line, facing the other. The players then number off from right to left.

In the center of the space between the lines there is a rock with a handkerchief on it.

One player, chosen to be the leader, calls a number. The players on each side who have that number run out to the center. If one gets there first, he snatches up the handkerchief and dashes back to his line. He will be safe and score two points for his side if he reaches the line without being tagged. The other player tries to tag him before he reaches it. If the other player succeeds in tagging him, it scores one point for his side.

Very often both runners reach the rock at the same instant. When this happens, each one tries to wait until he has a good chance to get a head start before snatching the handkerchief. Each runs in, pretends to grab for the handkerchief, and does everything possible to get his opponent a little way away from the rock.

One thing is important. Don't touch the handkerchief while you are pretending to grab for it. If you touch it, even though you don't pick it up, the other player can tag you and score a point.

HOP ACROSS

To play "Hop Across," the players divide into two equal teams, and each team marks a goal line on the ground. The two goal lines should be about 25 feet apart.

Each team lines up along its own goal line. Then, at the signal to start, the two teams advance toward each other with arms folded across their chests, all players hopping on one leg. The object of the game for each player is to try to cross the other side's goal line without being forced to put his lifted foot on the ground.

Some players go after each other, trying to bump or shoulder members of the other team to force them off balance, so they will have to put their foot down. Other players may do their best to keep out of trouble and make for the opposite goal line as quickly as possible.

The team that gets the greatest number of players across the other side's goal line is the winner.

CROSS TAG

One player is "It." He begins to chase a player, and once started, he must keep after this player until he catches him or—and this is where the fun comes in —until some other player dashes between "It" and the runner. When this happens, "It" has to chase the new runner who crossed between him and his quarry.

As the game goes on, all the players take advantage of every opportunity to cross between "It" and the player he is chasing. In this way everybody gets actively into the game.

SNAKE AND BIRDS

Ten or more players are needed for this unusual game. Eight or more boys make a chain by holding hands in a line. They are the Snake. The girls, who are the Birds, scatter at some distance from the Snake.

The Snake starts looking for the Birds, and when it gets close to one it tries to catch the Bird by making a circle around her. The Bird runs as fast as she can, trying to get out of the circle before it closes around her. As soon as the boys at either end of the chain join hands, the Bird is caught.

When a Bird is caught, she drops out of the game.

DRAGON'S TAIL

There should be at least eight players for "Dragon's Tail," but an unlimited number can take part in the game.

The players are divided into two equal groups, and each team makes a "dragon" by getting in a line, all facing the same way. Each player holds the waist of the one in front of him.

The last player in each line has a handkerchief waving in back from his belt. This is the dragon's tail. The object of the game is for the first player of each dragon to try to get the other dragon's tail. It takes a lot of running and dodging to protect the two rear men.

Play for points, each dragon scoring one point for each time it succeeds in getting the other dragon's tail.

FIRE IN THE MOUNTAIN

You need about fifteen players for this game, which is one of the running and dashing kind. It is good at a picnic or any other kind of outdoor party.

All the players, except the one who is "It," divide into two equal groups. The players of one group stand in a wide circle. The players in the second group then form an outer circle by standing in back of the players in the first circle. "It" stand in the center of the inner circle.

"It" starts things going by calling out, "Fire in the mountain! Run, boys, run!" At this command the second group of players start to run around the inner circle. They may run fast or slow.

Also, at "Its" command, the players in the inner circle and "It" himself start to clap their hands in rhythm.

Suddenly, without warning, "It" stops clapping and puts his hands up over his head. The players in the inner circle all do the same. Immediately each player in the outer circle dashes to try to get in front of a player in the inner circle. "It" also runs to get a place in front of one of these players. The person who is left out becomes "It" and goes to the center.

ELBOW TAG

This is one of the best of all the tag games, and one that may be new to you. It is fast and full of excitement.

The players divide up into couples—two boys, two girls, or a boy and a girl, depending on who is in the group. One couple then volunteers to be "It."

The other couples stand about fifteen feet apart with elbows linked. All the players put their free hands on their hips, so the elbows jut out at an angle.

One of the two players who are "It" now starts to chase the other, after giving him a good head start. They run close to the others, weaving in and out among them. At any time the player who is being chased may hook onto the free elbow of any other player.

When this happens, that player's partner must free his elbow and run, because *he* is now being chased. If the chaser tags the player he is chasing before the latter links onto someone's elbow, the tables are turned. The one who was being chased at once becomes the chaser.

CROWS AND CRANES

"Crows and Cranes" is a good game to play at a picnic. You need a fairly big open space in which to play it.

The players are divided into two equal teams. One is the Crows and the other is the Cranes. One player, who is not on either team, is the leader. The leader stands in the center and the teams line up along their goal lines. These are sixty to eighty feet apart.

The leader calls, "O.K. Get going," and both teams start to walk slowly forward toward the center. When they are fairly close to him, the leader calls the name of one of the teams—Crows or Cranes. A good leader rolls out Cr-cr-r-r-r-r-r as long as he can, in order to keep both sides in suspense.

When the leader finally names one of the teams, that team turns around and runs for its goal line. The other team chases it and tries to tag as many of its players as possible. Those who are tagged have to join the other side. No player may be tagged in back of his own goal line.

The leader, if he wishes to, may put the names of the teams into sentences, such as "I hear the sound of cr-cr-r-r-r-r-cracking and cr-cr-r-r-r-r-crunching. A cr-cr-r-r-r-cracker is being eaten by a big cr-r-r-r-crazy—CRANE." This makes the game more exciting. The leader may also let the teams get very close together before calling Crows or Cranes.

The game is over when one side has caught all the members of the other side.

POISON BALL

Everybody stands in a circle, except "It," who is in the center. He has a rubber ball, a tennis ball or a beach ball. He turns around slowly, looking at each player in the circle, and moving as though about to throw the ball at someone. If anyone starts to dodge or jump, he is out. And, when "It" does throw the ball and hits someone below the knees, that player is out.

Usually a good many players go out by jumping when "It" pretends that he is going to throw the ball at them. They know that they have to move fast to avoid being hit, if "It" really does throw the ball.

I SPY

This is another old favorite that never seems to lose its popularity.

One player is chosen to be "It." He covers his eyes with his hands and, standing by a tree or rock serving as home base, counts, "Five, ten, fifteen, twenty," and so on, until he reaches one hundred. All the other players scatter and hide. When "It" reaches one hundred, he uncovers his eyes and shouts: "Here I come! Ready or not!"

He then tries to find the other players. When he sees one he shouts: "I spy Bill," or whoever it is, and runs for home base. If the other player reaches home before "It" does, he is safe. The first player beaten to home base by "It" becomes "It" for the next game.

The game can stop after "It" returns to home base before the first player, or can keep on until the last player has run for home, with "It" trying to beat him to it. In either case, the first player whom "It" beats home is "It" for the next game.

KING OF THE CASTLE

One player is chosen King. He immediately gets busy and finds a little mound or a stump to be his castle. If there is no natural castle, you can mark off a circle on the ground.

Once safely installed in his castle, the King shouts at all the other players, calling out:

"I'm the King of the castle,
Get out, you cowardly rascal."

At this, the excitement starts, as everybody rushes up to the castle and tries to push or pull the King out of it. You can push and you can grab the King's hands and pull, but you are not allowed to catch hold of his clothes. If you do this, you immediately become a prisoner of war and have to leave the game.

It takes a pretty powerful King to stay in the castle for more than a few minutes. The player who succeeds in getting him out becomes the next King.

DODGE BALL

"Dodge Ball" is most fun when you have between ten and twenty players.

The players start by counting off. The odd-numbered players then form an outer circle, and the even-numbered ones go inside the circle. The players in the outer circle try to hit those inside with any sort of soft ball.

The ball must be aimed low, below the waists of the inside players. When a player is hit, he joins the outside circle. The outside players try to fool the others now and then by passing or tossing the ball to each other and by pretending to throw the ball in one direction and actually throwing it somewhere else. The last inside player to be hit is the winner.

The game is also played in another way. Five players go inside the circle and hold each other's waists to form a chain. The players in the circle then try to hit the last man in the chain with the ball. When the end man is hit he joins the circle, and the player who hit him becomes the first man of the chain.

The object of the first man of the chain, and the others in the chain also, is to keep the chain moving so that the end man is kept away from the player who is about to throw the ball. This calls for continuous dodging and swinging about.

171

PRISONER'S BASE

There should be at least ten players to play "Prisoner's Base," and the game is even better when there are more.

The players divide into two equal teams. Then two lines are drawn, one by each team. These lines may be from twenty to sixty feet apart. In back of each line

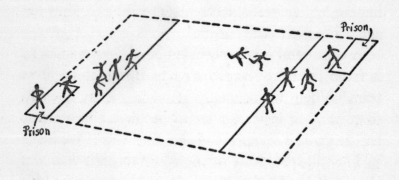

a box is marked out, measuring about ten feet by five feet. These boxes are the prisons. They are usually placed in the positions shown in the drawing.

The game starts with one team's sending a player out into No Man's Land, between the two lines, to dare the other side. A player from the other side starts at once to chase him. If this opponent tags the player before he gets back to his line, the player becomes a Prisoner and must go to the other side's prison. He may be saved from being tagged by a teammate who runs out and tags the opponent or chases him back to his own line.

There is just one important rule: a player may tag any opponent who left his base line before he did himself.

When a player has tagged an opponent, he is allowed to walk back to his own base line without being tagged. He may be tagged only after he runs out again into No Man's Land.

A captured player must remain in prison until he is freed by being tagged by a member of his own team. When this happens, both players are allowed to go back to their own line. No one is permitted to tag them.

The rule is that a Prisoner has to keep only one foot in prison. He may reach out to make his rescue by a teammate easier. When there are several Prisoners, they can form a line, and the player at the rear end of the line keeps one foot in the prison. But only one Prisoner—the one at the head of the line—can be freed at one time.

The game keeps up until one team has captured all the other side or, as often happens, until everybody is exhausted and ready to call it a day.

POM POM PULLAWAY

This is one of the most popular of all outdoor games.

About thirty feet apart, two lines are clearly marked on the ground with stones and sticks or by making two shallow furrows with a stick.

All the players except "It" then stand behind one of the lines. He stands in the center, between the lines, and calls out:

"Pom Pom Pullaway!
If you don't come, I'll pull you away."

All the players must run like mad for the other line. "It" tries to tag as many as he can. Each player tagged joins forces with "It" and tries to tag other players. The game keeps on until every player has been caught. Then the first one tagged becomes "It" for the next game.

SOAKEY

Whoever gets the idea that it would be fun to play "Soakey" starts by calling out, "Soakey, one ender." Another player then shouts, "Soakey, two ender." These two players are the end men. They put their handkerchiefs on the ground some distance apart.

174

The other players then place their handkerchiefs in a straight line between those of the two end men.

Each player stands beside his handkerchief. One of the end players rolls a rubber ball or tennis ball, hoping it will stop on one of the handkerchiefs. If it does, the excitement starts.

The player on whose handkerchief the ball lands picks up the ball immediately and throws it, trying to hit some other player. By this time the others have run away as far and as fast as possible. If a player is hit, he ties a stone in his handkerchief. If the thrower misses, he puts a stone in his own handkerchief.

The game goes on until some player has three stones in his handkerchief. When this happens, the losing player has to stand bent over against a tree, while all the others stand twenty feet away and try to "soak" him with the ball.

LAME WOLF

Mark off a space at one end of the playing field for the den of the Lame Wolf. Then mark off another space at the opposite end of the field to be the home of the other players. They are the Children the Wolf is out to get.

One of the players is chosen to be the Lame Wolf,

and goes into the den. The Children run out of their house and go fairly close to the den, shouting, "Who's afraid of the big, bad wolf?" and "Lame Wolf's no good. He can't catch anybody."

The Wolf watches closely, and the moment he thinks he has a chance of catching someone, rushes out of his den. However, he is lame, so he can run only three steps and then must hop on one foot. This means that he must use all his skill and cunning to lure the children close in to his den.

Players who are caught become Lame Wolves, and start in to help catch the others. Each time, after someone is caught, all the Children go home and the Lame Wolves retire to their den. Then the children start the next round by approaching the den and jeering at the poor Lame Wolves.

POISONED ROCK

There should be ten or twelve players in this game. Mark a circle on the ground about five feet in diameter. In the middle of the circle put a fairly large rock. The players then stand in a ring around the edge of the circle holding each other's hands. Each player tries to keep from touching the rock and to pull some of the other players inside the circle and make them touch the poisoned rock. The players push and pull each other, trying to throw each other off balance and into the circle.

When a player touches the rock, he is out of the game. The others go on playing until there is a stalemate or until only one player is left.

STATUES

Five to ten players are a good number for "Statues," though more can play if there is a large group.

A starting line is marked on the ground and all the players except "It" stand at the line. "It" stands about twenty feet in front of the line. He turns around so that his back is toward the others.

"It" calls out, "Ready, go!" and starts counting to ten. He must count so everybody can hear him, and he may count slow or fast. While he is counting, the others walk or run toward him. But when he reaches ten, they all turn into statues. They stand absolutely still, even if they have one foot off the ground.

At the count of ten, "It" turns quickly around and calls out the names of any players whom he catches moving. These players must go back to the starting line and begin over again.

"It" then counts again. Finally some player will

get close enough to run in and tag "It" while he is counting. Then all the players run for the starting line, and "It" dashes after them. If "It" tags some player before he crosses the line, that player becomes "It." But if "It" fails to tag someone, he must continue being "It."

SQUIRREL IN A TREE

This is a tag game, with some special features that make it unusually exciting.

Two players are chosen to be the Dog and the Squirrel. The other players form groups of three. In each group, two players face each other and hold hands to form a "Tree." The third player stands between them, inside the Tree.

When all the Trees are ready, the Dog starts to chase the Squirrel. When the Dog gets too close, the Squirrel can save himself by ducking down and getting into a Tree. The player already in the Tree then becomes the Squirrel and has to run away as fast as he can.

The more often the Squirrel changes, the more the excitement; so if you are the Squirrel, don't hesitate to duck into a Tree even though the Dog may not be breathing right down your neck.

When the Dog catches a Squirrel, that Squirrel becomes the Dog. He starts out by chasing the previous Dog, who usually ducks into the first Tree he comes to, in order to catch his breath and get a little rest.

NAME TOSS

A circle about 20 feet in diameter is marked on the ground. All the players, except the one who is "It," stand around the edge of the circle.

"It" stands in the middle and throws a baseball or tennis ball as high as he can up into the air. The moment the ball leaves his hand, he calls the name of one of the other players. This player must try to catch the ball.

If he fails, he is out of the game and must leave the circle, sit down, and take it easy. The game keeps on until only one player is left in the ring. He is the winner and becomes "It" for the next game.

Every throw has to land inside the circle. If one lands outside, the player whose name was called doesn't have to catch it.

FIGHTER PLANES

"Fighter Planes" is played by four players at a time, and creates plenty of excitement. It is like an air battle fought on the ground.

To play it, two lengths of clothesline or strong string are needed, each about ten feet long. Two of the players are Pilots and the other two are Fighters. The two Fighters are blindfolded, and each one is given a newspaper rolled up to serve as a swatter. The Pilots then harness the Fighters with rope. This is done by doubling the rope and placing the center point, where it forms a loop, at the back of the Fighter's neck. Then the rope is brought down over each shoulder and under the armpits.

The Pilots take hold of the rope ends and bring their Fighters to within ten feet of each other. Now the game starts. The Pilots guide their Fighters by means of the ropes. If the Pilot shakes the rope up and down, the Fighter goes straight ahead. If the Pilot pulls on the rope that passes under the Fighter's right arm, the Fighter must move on an angle to the right. A pull on the left-hand rope steers the Fighter to the left. If the Pilot pulls with equal force on both ends of the rope, it is a signal to the Fighter to go backwards.

The Pilot's goal is to guide his Fighter to the best position from which to hit the other Fighter with his swatter. When this time comes, the Pilot signals the

Fighter to strike by pulling twice with equal force on both sides of the rope.

The game calls for skill and good timing—also for silence on the part of the Fighters. The Fighters must be quick to follow the signals, and the Pilots must give the right signals at the right time. Once they make contact, the Fighters can have a battle royal, but the Pilots can withdraw their men and maneuver for another strike whenever they want to.

HIT THE BAT

This game is played with a bat and a soft ball.

All the players except the batter stand in line in a group. The batter stands about twenty or twenty-five feet away from them. One player pitches the ball toward the batter, who hits the ball toward the other players and then puts the bat on the ground parallel to the line of the group.

The player who stops the ball now rolls it toward the bat. If he hits the bat, he becomes the batter. If he misses, the first batter bats again.

If a player catches the ball on the fly, he becomes the batter at once, without having to try to hit the bat. For this reason, the batter usually hits the ball toward the ground.

FOX AND GEESE

This is a favorite game to play in the snow. It is a very exciting chasing game.

A circle about twenty feet across is trampled out in the snow. Then six spokes are made, leading into a center circle, which is the goal.

One player is the Fox and the others are the Geese. The Fox chases the Geese, trying to tag them. If he does tag someone, the tagged player becomes the Fox, and the old Fox joins the other Geese in the circle.

The rule is that the Geese have to keep to the paths —the wheel and the spokes. If a Goose runs outside of the paths, he automatically becomes the Fox. The Geese may jump across from one path to another, but the Fox isn't allowed to. And, any Goose who stands in the center is safe.

However, only one Goose at a time is safe in the center. If there are two Geese in the center, the Fox may tag the one who got there first. If there are more than two, the Fox may tag all except the last one to enter the center—that is, unless the others run away before he can catch them.

CHAIN TAG

Two lines are marked on the ground about fifty feet apart. All the players except "It" stand behind one of the lines.

When "It" calls out "Run!" all the other players must try to get across the center space and reach the other line. "It" tries to tag as many as he can. All the players whom "It" tags join hands with him at once and help him in tagging others.

In this way, a chain of players is formed, all holding hands. The two end players of the chain are the only ones allowed to do the tagging. The tagged players may take their places in the chain on either side of "It."

"It" calls "Run!" every time all the untagged players are safe behind a line. The game usually lasts until all the players have been caught. Then the first player who was tagged becomes "It" for the next game.

At the sides of the center space there must be definite out-of-bounds lines, either marked out or identified in some other way. This is necessary to keep players from running far away from the playing area between the two lines.

NO MAN'S LAND

This is a very popular outdoor game, but you can play it indoors too, if you have a big enough room and clear the furniture out of the way.

The players are divided into two equal teams, and a line is marked on the ground or on the floor. The teams stand close to the line on opposite sides of it.

At the signal to start, the players of each team try to pull the opposing players over the line. Several players may gang up on one player on the other team and try to pull him bodily over the line. But at the same time, the player's teammates may hang onto him and try to keep him from slipping over into the enemy's territory. Almost anything goes, as long as it is fair. Players must not step over the line. If one does, he is out of the game right away.

There are two ways to play this game: a player is either out when he is pulled over the line, or he joins the other side and helps them against his original teammates.

BACK TO BACK

"Back to Back" is a good running game in which there is a lot of dashing about. You should have at least ten players to make it the most fun.

The players stand in pairs in a big circle. "It" is in the center of the circle. "It" first calls "Back to back!" and each pair of players stands back to back. Then "It" calls "Face to face!" and each pair must face each other and shake hands.

"It" next calls "Back to back!" This time—and each time afterwards that he calls "Back to back!"— all the players must change partners. During the scramble "It" tries to get a partner. He usually succeeds, because so many people are running at the same time, and the player who is left out becomes "It."

Index

187

188

189

guess-the-name

stick-jumping race

who is the leader?

huckle-buckle